A handbook of

SCHOOL

BULLYING

Mathamsanqa Ndlovu Lutango

Dedication

For Nicky

Contents

Acknowledgements

To all my family and friends who never stopped believing in me.

CHAPTER 1

THE PROBLEM OF BULLYING IN SCHOOLS

This book was inspired by a research carried in the rural town of Port St Johns in the Eastern Cape province of South Africa. Before the study was conceptualized, as a teacher I had witnessed bullying among learners on a daily basis I heard stories reported by learners, of people being mean to others. Not once off events but events which were repeatedly carried out to inflict pain on the less powerful victims. In one incident a grade 7 boy reported that his hat had been taken away by another boy who was also in grade seven. Apparently it wasn't the first time something like this had happened. He (the bully) had taken the victim's hat before and he never returned it later he was seen wearing it at his neighborhood and no one could ask for it because he belonged to a gang of sorts probably made up of bullies like him. When he took the second hat he had actually told the other learners early in the morning that that the victim wouldn't go with his hat home. Sure enough when they came back from first break the hat was missing from the victims' school bag. The bully had taken it, but of course he denied having taken it. When reported to teachers he maintained his story.

However two weeks later a tiny grade 6 boy who had witnessed the incident came to report to me that he had seen the bully wearing the hat at the location thereafter he swore me into secrecy. It was disturbing that learners could get away with such behaviour at the expense of others. At least some witnesses had the guts to report the bullying, but my main worry was that teachers either ignored bullying or saw it as part of growing up or didn't know how to handle the situations because they themselves are sometimes victims of bullying.

In every school I learnt as a child I witnessed bullying and was once victim of it. I saw and heard of severe forms of bullying especially among boys. Real mean stuff that scared me out of my wits. I also witnessed a lot of indirect bullying aimed at isolating an individual. Most adults have witnessed such stuff and now it could even be worse because there is cyber bullying in social networks, cellphones etc which is more hidden but which our kids are getting exposed to. So it's not just the bullies giving you a hard time at school but they follow you home on your cellphone or computer. Hence parents, guardians, teachers and learners need to be enlightened about the very nature of bullying and how it can be dealt with. If I had the knowledge I have now, when I was a learner am sure I would have been in a better position to deal with the kids who bullied me and my friends.

Going to school: parents and children's dreams and wishes

Day one of school in January 2013 I watched the news coverage of inland provinces as they opened schools. Children interviewed all seemed to be looking forward to the start of the long journey to matric. Some parents told the news reporter that their kids had woken up as early as four o'clock and had shown a great deal of excitement. Except for a few who had a hard time being separated from their parents for the first time, the children generally seemed happy to be in grade 1 for the first time. The long awaited journey had finally begun both for the parent and the child. The child goes to school expecting to learn almost everything if not all that the teacher will teach. Parents likewise consumed by the excitement of the first day of school, forget the reality of the school context or at least expect that their kids will fit in well and rise above situations if need be. On that particular day no one anticipates that their child will be a victim of some mean behavior amounting to bullying, or worse still that their child will become the perpetrator of repeated hurtful acts on other children.

The reality of the school context

The true reality is that it happens and children can be the perpetrators, the victims or even onlookers. At school kids meet different characters some of which show a tendency to dominate others, some seem to fail to stand up to others (for whatever reason) and some still seem to be prone towards showing provocative behaviour, others do not want to get on the wrong side of the dominant ones so they avoid the bullies, some help the bullies and others watch from afar and do not want to intervene for fear of becoming the next 'culprit'. Better still others intervene to stop this nonsense. All these characters play their roles in either abating or perpetrating the bullying cycle. And children can take any role with or without the knowledge of their 2parents, teachers or any other responsible adults in their schools. True enough children have their tiffs and fights and these are only normal if they occur between equal peers of the same height, age, strength etc. and both parties have an equal chance of winning the fight. However if one party has an upper hand or advantage over the other and uses their position to repeatedly inflict harm on the other who cannot fight back the bullying has begun. Bullying at school can begin on the first day of the new year or it can start when kids have gotten used to each other and somewhat have a feel of how and what things are done at school. Several other factors may play a role on how and when bullying starts besides the school context.

Adjusting to the school setting

In his theory of evolution, Charles Darwin explains the concept of 'better adapted, of the immediate' commonly called the 'survival of the fittest'. This does not necessarily refer to the fittest in terms of physical strength or appearance because there are bullies who are tiny in stature and victims who are big. Rather it refers to how one mentally adjusts to the environment to survive in this case to avoid being bullied or to stop the bully from harassing them. Adjustment to the school setting can be negative or positive and is sometimes influenced by the culture of the school. Schools have what is called the hidden curriculum which refers to activities and behaviours which are acceptable even though they are not written down. There are unwritten norms which the teachers follow or allow even though they do not approve of them and bullying is one such. Bullying can occur in a school because there is a permissive attitude for bullying among learners and teachers or it may not occur because there is no permissive attitude. So how one adjusts or fails to is largely dependent on their character, how they handle disputes with other learners and how the school operates in terms of the hidden curriculum. For example when I went to high school at a boarding school there was an unwritten norm that juniors must be 'welcomed in a special way' which was bullying. Some of which was perpetrated by prefects and teachers. Seniors had this misconception that they had to orient new students and the tradition was carried on year after year. The administration only seemed to attend to serious bullying like when people got physically hurt or sick (especially from the boys' side).

So how does bullying start?

Some victims can recall how and when they were first bullied while some cannot, depending on the nature of bullying. Normally bullying starts when one child or children repeatedly do things that are hurtful or harm another. This one person or group of people begins to exercise their power on another child who seemingly fails to give adequate response to make the bully or bullies back off. Once the bully sees that the victim cannot stand up to him or her then the bullying starts and it can spiral out of control making the victim's life greatly unbearable at school.

Why write about bullying?

Besides carrying out research about bullying in my studies, bullying has always been a cause for concern to me as a teacher and a parent. For the most part of my life I did not know how to really define bullying. I didn't even know that some actions or behaviours became bullying once they were done repeatedly. The aim of this book is to raise awareness to anyone who reads it about what bullying is what it entails and how it can be dealt with at school level.

The problem of bullies in schools

Recent studies show that bullying is a common problem with many children and adolescents in both western and non-western countries [86]. Bullying occurs among children worldwide and has been a long standing problem and it has even been described in fictional works for centuries [44]. It should therefore be acknowledged as a possible problem before it can be tackled (65). Media reports also show that bullying is a problem not only for learners but for teachers as well. More than 50% of teachers report being bullied at school [31].

In an article published by Jindrinch Ginter, in the Czech internet daily Britske` Listy on 12 June 2000 [10], he outlined the horrific bullying events that occur at school. He stated that bullying occurs relatively often and approximately 20% of children in Czech schools are bullied. In the same article Michal Koler, a specialist in abnormal behaviour who provides support for psychologists and the police at the Czech Police Academy reported some of the following cases which are reportedly encountered in Czech schools: victims are forced to drink urine, to drink lemonade which other people have spat on, they are forced to eat from the ground, they are forced to masturbate in public, kiss other learners' shoes or to clean them and they are also forced to kneel down and beg for mercy.

In cases of hanging, children are being hung by the neck until they lose consciousness. They are choked with cable, rope or plastic bags, cushions or towels and it is timed how long a victim can breathe. Victims are 'pretend play' thrown out of the window, bottoms pricked with sharp knives, pins and so on and darts are thrown at living targets. Victims are stripped naked and flogged, they are mocked. There is mass kicking or anonymous mass beatings of a single person, punching the victim's stomach, slaps or hitting the victim on the neck, forcing victims to fight 'gladiator games', cutting or burning the victims' hair, threatening the victim with death, anonymous telephone call threats and intimidating the victims with weapons.

The article also cited one incident where the bullying culminated to veritable lynching of a 14 year old girl who was lured to the forest, was beaten up, stripped naked, kicked, whipped with nettles and forced to spread human excrement on her face.

In South Africa, the Sunday Times published an article about exposing bullies who make teens' lives hell on 22 April 2012, where a TV presenter outlined his ordeal with bullies who used to wait for him by the toilet and told him to pay R1 to urinate and R2 for number two. In the same article Dr. Crystal Watson who carried out a study about bullying stated that bullying in South Africa is becoming an epidemic. Children she had interviewed told how they had been thrown to the ground, kicked, thrown in dustbins and stripped of their clothing. As a result they feared going to school, were withdrawn and lost their self-esteem.

The article also cited the following incidents of bullying: a cellphone video footage that went viral earlier in 2012. It showed a 15 year old girl being hit over the head with a glass bottle over the head. The 70 second clip also showed four high school girls calling the teenager fat and throwing diet pills at her. The article also reported other incidents of cyber bullying which include the circulation of a 'slut-list' on the cell phone group Mxit. The names and telephone numbers of the 'sluts' were on the list.

As a form of aggression among children bullying is not a new phenomena yet it has detrimental consequences that can last for a long time [2].The school is one such place where bullying is very prevalent and poses serious challenges to everyone involved in the 14schooling system. In schools bullying occurs among and between both boys and girls [31]. The school environment presents children with challenges that require them to negotiate and renegotiate relationships, self-image and independence. They cultivate interpersonal skills, discover and refine strengths and struggle with vulnerabilities [23]. They have to develop friendships and learn to give a suitable response to the bully. These responses could be totally avoiding or ignoring the bully, turning the prank around so that it makes the 'pranksteree' out of the would be prankster and even summoning legal intervention [12]. Those who fail to cultivate interpersonal skills and overcome vulnerabilities can be subjected to bullying.

The prevalence rates of bullying in schools are very high. The prevalence of victimization in grades one to five varies from a low of 11,3% in a sample of learners in Finland [62] to a high of 49,8% in a nationwide study in Ireland [19].According to the First South Africa national youth risk behavior survey the Department of Health (2002), [21] , 49,3% of secondary school learners in Free State reported that they had been bullied in the month preceding the survey.

In schools bullying can occur in any part of the premises such as play grounds, classrooms, corridors, hallways and even in school buses and waiting for buses [31]. It may even occur in classes that require group work or after school activities [21]. It has also been found to be prevalent at school or when the child is traveling to or from school [46].

Research on bullying began with studies carried in the 1970s, by the Norwegian researcher Dan Olweus [59]. Internationally, extensive research on bullying has been carried out in Europe, Australia, and North America.

In the United States of America, researchers [55] conducted a national study of 15,686 students in grade 6 through grade 10. They reported that nearly 30% of students indicated more than occasional involvement as a bully and/ victim of bullying. Males were more frequently involved as both bullies and victims, as were students in grades six through eight. In addition, Hispanic students reported slightly higher involvement as bullies than white or African - American students, while African - American students reported being bullied less frequently than both white and Hispanic students. Lastly more students from rural areas reported bullying than did individuals from suburban and urban areas.

In the Netherlands, a study examined the extent to which classroom factors (i.e., classroom anti-bullying attitudes and behavioural norms) contributed to individual bullying after controlling for individual difference characteristics. They found that adolescents in classrooms that held permissive attitudes toward bullying were more likely to bully themselves, even after controlling for bullying attitude, gender, social preference and number of reciprocal friends. They eventually concluded that the effects of classroom antibullying attitudes might be partly mediated by classroom behaviour [86].

In Nigeria a study examined the psychopathology of bullying and emotional abuse among school children [3]. The study was carried out in private and public schools in Lagos, including boarders and non-boarders aged between 12 and 19. They found that the incidence of bullying was more pronounced among boys and girls who were day students compared to those who were boarders. Their study showed that frequent bullying is a predicting factor for anxiety disorder in early adulthood and victims of bullying experience more physical and psychological problems than their peers who are not harassed by others.

Several studies have been carried out in South Africa by, among others, where letters were written to newspapers and readers were invited to share their experiences with regard to bullying. Readers pointed out that bullying resulted in, for instance, low self-image and went on to describe how their lives had been permanently affected by this scourge [47].

In one study [59] about peer victimisation among learners between grade 6 and grade 11, in schools in Gauteng it was established that most of the learners had been subjected to milder forms of bullying such as teasing and name-calling. More serious bullying occurred less frequently. Direct physical assault among male learners was very high and fifty percent of bullying was done by a learner. A study found bullying in an upmarket school in Gauteng to be very rife. The study unequivocally revealed the need for safety in authoritarian schools as a result of bullying [48].

The nature and prevalence of bullying in intermediate phase in was studied in Bloemfontein Metropolis in Free State [35]. This study established a very high incidence of bullying among intermediate phase learners. The greater proportion of learners (both girls and boys) reported being bullied by learners in their own classes. Another bullying study in some Free State schools revealed that not only verbal and physical, but sexual bullying is pervasive and serious in some Free State schools [23].

Other South African studies have investigated whether bullying behavior predicts high school dropout, and the trend has been that girls who were both bullies and victims were found to be at greater risk for dropping out of school [96]. It has also been established that some girls have innate characteristics which protect them from bullying and the environment also plays a part in either maintaining bullying or protecting learners from bullying [93]. Some authors [51] found that in the Eastern Cape Province the geographical area was significantly associated with bullying status and achieving higher grades than classmates was significantly associated with victimisation as were rewards for conventional involvement in school.

Academic literature (especially in journals) on bullying has grown significantly since the 1980s, there are a few books that have been published about this phenomenon from an African or South African perspective. There is limited research about bullying in rural schools in South Africa. Although quite a considerable number of studies have been carried out in the western countries they focus on general bullying at school. Even among these studies the effects of bullying is still a relatively unresearched area. if parents, teachers and other stakeholders are knowledgeable about the reality and nature of bullying in schools, they will be better equipped to deal with the problem of bullying.

Definition of terms

Bullying –an intentional attempt by a learner to gain power or dominance over another learner, by committing repeated, unprovoked hurtful acts which can cause physical or emotional pain.

Bully- a child who deliberately inflicts pain, hurts or intimidates another child repeatedly.

Victim- a learner who has suffered repeated physical or emotional attacks from other learners.

Bystanders –"children who are neither victims nor perpetrators, but who see bullying happening to their peers" [48].Bystanders aid or abet the bully through their acts of omission and commission [17]. For the purposes of this study, bystanders will be defined as children who witness school bullying.

School- an organization or establishment where children acquire academic knowledge and learn how to live peacefully with other people.

School bullying- is "psychological, emotional, social or physical harassment of one student by another at school or within the school community. This includes the school and within its grounds, transit between school and home, local shopping centres, at parties or local parks and in cyberspace" [31].

In this book, school bullying will be defined as bullying which occurs in school premises and in related activities outside the school. It can even occur at home through cellphones social networks. As long as it is bullying done by one learner on another learner, in any context that links them to the school, it is school bullying. So if your child is receiving hurtful texts or blogs at home from fellow school mates then the school authorities should be notified because it is school related therefore it is school bullying.

CHAPTER 2
WHAT IS BULLYING?

Bullying is defined as when a learner is "exposed, repeatedly and over time, to negative actions on the part of one or more other learners. These negative actions are considered to be bullying when someone intentionally inflicts, or attempts to inflict injury or discomfort on another person"[66].

As noted above, bullying is also defines "as intentional, repeated hurtful acts, words or other behavior such as name-calling, threatening or shunning, committed by a child or children against another child or children" [17]. Bullying occurs repeatedly over time and involves an on going pattern of harassment, intimidation and abuse [3]. Bullying also constitutes an imbalance of power which may be physical, psychological or intellectual and causes an obstacle for victims to defend [11]. Bullying is also referred to as premeditated continuous, malicious and belittling tyranny [22]. Bullying, therefore, can be said to be:

- Intentional;

- an attempt to gain power and dominance over another person;

- planed beforehand;

- a conscious act;

- done repeatedly; and

constitutes an imbalance of power which can be physical, psychological or intellectual.

Forms of bullying

The US National Center for Education Statistics [56] states that school bullying can be classified into two categories namely direct bullying and indirect bullying which is also known as social aggression. Direct bullying involves a great deal of physical aggression while indirect bullying or social aggression is characterized by threatening the victim into social isolation [83]. Direct/physical bullying can be easily identified while indirect or social bullying is generally covert, thereby rendering it invisible [93].That is, bullying may be overt or covert.

❖ *Direct/physical bullying-* is face-to-face bullying in which students confront each other in person [98]. Direct bullying involves a great deal of physical aggression such as shoving and poking, throwing things, slapping, choking, punching and kicking, beating, stabbing, pulling hair, scratching, biting, scraping and pinching. It can also include pushing, stabbing with sharp objects, taking other peoples' belongings by force, stealing things from other's bags, damaging clothes or stationary, forcing others to fight, and throwing things at others [83].

❖ *Indirect relational/social bullying-* involves purposeful actions that lead to social exclusion or damage to a child's status or reputation in an attempt to get others not to socialize with the victim [22]. Other forms of indirect bullying are more subtle and more likely to be verbal , such as name calling , the silent treatment , arguing others into submission , manipulation , gossip/false gossip, lies, rumors/false rumors, staring, giggling, laughing at the victim, saying certain words that trigger a reaction from a past event and mocking. Social aggression or indirect bullying is characterized by threatening the victim into social isolation. This isolation is achieved through a wide variety of techniques, including gossip, refusing to socialize with the victim, and criticizing the victim's manner of dress and other socially significant markers (including the victim's race, religion, disability, sex, sexual preference etc.).social or indirect bullying can also include teasing, hurtful name calling, exclusion from activities like games, threats to give money or other things, staring, making faces, making fun of others and mocking [83].

The medium of school bullying may be face to face bullying in which students confront each other in person or it can be cyber bullying [97].

- ❖ *Cyber bullying-* Cyber bullying takes place online via email, chartrooms, social networking sites, blogs, text messages, instant messages, website postings and more. Often cyber bullying is done anonymously as the bullies conceal their identities and the victim experiences anonymous attacks. Cyber bullying may include the victim becoming ganged up on, in a series of bashing and hurtful statements. It may consist of all the types of content mentioned in emotional bullying above, including insulting and derogatory comments about someone or sending such comments to someone, sending mean or threatening messages, gossiping about someone online, including posting sensitive or private information, impersonating someone in order to cast that person in a bad light, and excluding someone from an online page or group [97].

Nature of bullying

The nature of bullying differs. In a school context bullying ranges from simple one-on-one bullying, to more complex bullying in which the bully may have one or more "lieutenants " who may seem to be willing to assist, the primary bully in his bullying activities [9]

The nature of bullying is determined by how many bullies are involved. There are generally two types of bullying; pack bullying and individual bullying.

- **Pack bullying**-is bullying undertaken by a group (**www.nces.org/bullying**). Pack bullying may be perpetrated in person or in cyber space .In person it can take place in school yards, school hallways, sports fields, gymnasiums, classrooms and on the school bus [106].The website also states that according to the 2009 Wesley report on bullying, prepared by an Australian based group, pack bullying was found to be more prominent in high schools and characteristically lasted longer than bullying undertaken by individuals.

- **Individual bullying-** individual bullying is one-on-one bullying that may take place either in person or online, as well as being physical bullying or emotional bullying (**www.nces.org/bullying**). The Wesley report found it to be more prevalent in elementary schools. It can take place everywhere that pack bullying can, and also in smaller areas into which a pack can't fit, such as bathrooms [106].

Gender of bullies

Both boys and girls can be bullies and victims [31]. Recent research asserts that boys are more likely than girls to be involved in direct/ physical bullying [6; 55], and both boys and girls are equally involved in indirect/social bullying. In addition, [31] posits that both boys and girls can be bullies and victims. She further points out that,

Boys-

- Bully both girls and boys.

- Bully more openly and experience more physical bullying and threats.

- Use bullying tactics to make a reputation and girls use bullying tactics to protect a reputation.

Girls-

- Generally bully other girls.

- Can be physical but generally prefer indirect methods such as verbal, emotional and social bullying.

- Use teasing, taunting, devaluing, isolation from the group and spreading malicious rumours to bully (all less obvious to teachers.)

Seemingly boys are more involved in direct/physical bullying which is overt to the teachers while girls seem to prefer indirect/social bullying which is more covert to the teachers. While boys can bully either sex, girls concentrate their bullying on other girls.

Prevalence of bullying

Previous research has established that bullying is very much existent in schools [16]. In South Africa, it was noted that there is an alarming increase in bullying activities in schools [36]. The bullying statistics of 2010 reveal that bullying is a crime that is not going soon. There are approximately 160 000 children who sometimes miss school out of fear of being bullied [31]. Worldwide it is estimated that up to 50% of children are faced with the complex social dilemma of bullying in schools, as either perpetrators or victims [93]. It is reported that bullying is even taking on a different approach with cyber bullying becoming more and more rampant in school and after school. Bullying among learners is a serious problem that needs thorough investigation in order to minimize (if not eradicate) it completely [17].

Bullying among students has been studied extensively for the past 30 years [50] and research on the prevalence of school bullying is very high and has occurred in both first world and third world countries. In Australia,[31] most children have either been bullied, bully others or witnessed bullying at school. She also states that more than five children are bullied regularly at school and about one in five children can bully. In the United States of America, the National Centre for Education Statistics (2011) report, reveals that there is noticeably more bullying in middle school grades (grades 6, 7 and 8) than in senior high school and emotional bullying is the most prevalent type of bullying, with pushing/shoving/tripping/spitting on someone being second.

The prevalence of victimization in grades one to five varies from a low of 11, 3% in a sample of learners in Finland [62] to a high of 49, 8% in a nationwide study in Ireland [19]. In Canada, bullying in a middle school affects between fifteen to twenty percent of learners [101]. A 2003 survey on cyber bullying in the USA found that 57% of the learner participants said that someone had said hurtful or nasty things to them on line, 13% saying it happened quite often [40]. 15% of the learners in primary and lower secondary schools between ages 7 through to 16 in Norway were involved in bully/victim problems with some regularity either as bullies or victims [66].

The rate of bullying among learners in South African schools could be much higher [22]. In a research project in Gauteng, 60, 9% of the 207 participants indicated that they were bullied during the 2002 school year [59]. According to the First South Africa national youth risk behavior survey (Department of Health, 2002) [22], 49, 3% of secondary school learners in Free State reported that they had been bullied in the month preceding the survey.

In a 1990 South African study of 1073 grade one and grade two learners, researchers found that thirty-eight percent of learners were bullied by peers [79]. In the study [51] in the Eastern Cape Province, South Africa, students reported that in the previous year, 3,9% were bullies, 16,49% were victims of bullying, and 5,35% were bully-victims. It is evident from the aforementioned research findings that bullying is very prevalent in schools and it affects a large number of learners.

Location of bullying

Bullying occurs in any school: small or large, single sex, co-educational, traditional and progressive. It occurs in primary, secondary, boarding school and tertiary institutions. School bullying occurs at school and within its grounds, in transit between school and home, local shopping and sporting centres, at parties or local parks and in cyberspace. The playground is the most common place for bullying to occur [31].

In schools bullying can occur in any part of the premises such as play grounds, classrooms, corridors, hallways and even in school buses and waiting for buses [21]. It may even occur in classes that require group work or after school activities Bullying is common on school play grounds, dormitories, hostels, in neighborhoods, and in homes throughout Nigeria [3]. Bullying seemingly occurs at unsupervised localities within and outside the schoolyard but at times it can go on very close to the teacher without noticing it [55].

CHAPTER 3

THE BULLYING TRIAD

Who are the role players in bullying?

When bullying occurs it involves two or more people or parties, the bully, the victim and the bystander(s).The bully Triad consists of the person who bullies others (bully),the person who receives bullying (victim) and the other people who observe bullying (the bystanders) [17].

The bully

The bully is the first role player in the bullying triad. The bully is the child or group of children who carry out the bullying behaviour. They victimize their friends or peers through willful, conscious and deliberate actions intended to induce fear [65]. There are four specific types of bullies [8].

- The physical bullies – who often kick, hit or shove others.

- Verbal bullies – who use words to harm others through name-calling, insulting, making racist comments or harsh teasing.

- Relational bullies – who often focus on excluding one person from their peer group and usually do so through verbal threats and spreading rumors,.

- Reactive bullies – who are often both bully and victim. Typically victims first, they respond to victimization with bullying behavior [50].

These four broad categories of bullies can be further divided into smaller groups which are as follows;

The aggressive bully- The aggressive bully is the type who is aggressive to everybody and does not target weaker victims in particular. They are insensitive, domineering and lacking in self-control, but contrary to the popular belief, they are also high in self-esteem. Aggressive bullies are the most common type of bully [71]. Aggressive bullies are motivated by power and the desire to dominate others. They are the socially connected bullies [82], who tend to demonstrate within-sex bullying as part of a struggle for dominance, particularly in the beginning of the school year or between transitions from one school to another, when the social hierarchy is in flux and unpopular children can be targeted [73].

Confident bullies- The confident bully has a large ego, an inflated sense of self and a sense of entitlement. He/she has no empathy for the targets of their bullying. This type of bully is often admired by teachers because of his or her powerful personality but does not have many friends [17]. He is the clever bully who has ingenious ways of masking his behavior and often people around this bully cannot believe that he is capable of such negative behavior [91]. They target children who are not likely to be defended [14].

The hyper-active bully- is one who struggles with academics and has very little social skills. Their reason for bullying is a result of an inability to read social cues and often react aggressively even to the slightest provocation [17]. Their aggressive behavior is apparently due to a misinterpretation of people's actions.

The passive bully- This type of bully engages in bullying in order to protect him or herself and to achieve status. They are socially marginalized bullies who continuously come into conflict with others, they run against the world. They are consistently identified as being at risk even from bullying and harassment by others [82]. Their aggression is impulsive and overly reactive to real or perceived slights. They do not initiate bullying but react to provocation.

*The social bully-*By using rumour, gossip, verbal taunts and shunning, this bully isolates his/her targets by excluding them from social activities. Often this type of bully is envious of the victims' positive qualities and generally has a poor sense of self, hidden behind exaggerated confidence and charm. This bully is manipulative and may act caring but it is often a deceptive tool used to get what he or she wants [17].

The fully armoured bully- This bully is often cool and detached towards peers but yet very charming and deceptive especially in front of adults. When no one will stop him this is the time he will bully. The type of effect which is observed in this bully is flat (cold and unfeeling). He/she is usually vindictive and vicious towards his/her target [17].

The bully-victim- Bully-victims have behavioral problems. They have comorbid, externalizing and internalizing problems, hold significantly negative attitudes and beliefs about themselves and others [18]. Their bullying behavior is retaliatory, in response to being bullied. They are called the the bullied-bully and because they strike out at those who have bullied them and at weaker children [17].

The bunch of bullies- The bunch of bullies is described [17] as a group of friends who collectively behave in a negative way towards a specific target. Usually they target someone they would like to exclude from a group or use as a scapegoat. The way in which each member of the group behaves is different to how they would behave if they were by themselves. The peer norms of the group force the group members to conform to group standards. Thus when members in a peer group are involved in bullying, the other members tend to take part [94].

*The gang of bullies-*The gang of bullies is a group of people who come together to form a strategic alliance in the pursuit of power, control and dominance. Initially the group is formed for members to feel as if they are part of a family of sorts and to fulfill the need to be respected and protected. The group members become devoted to their group even if it is to the detriment of other individuals [17].

All these bullies can be group into two types; the malicious, who have been born with psychopathic or sociopathic tendencies (their brains are wired differently to ordinary children e.g. they like hurting animals) and those who are basically non-malicious but use bullying behaviors. They think, it's a game;I can get away with it; it will make me popular; it does not hurt and everyone does it. They actually bully for the sake of bullying [31].

Characteristics of bullies

The characteristics of children who bully by stating that they tend to have average or above average self-esteem and they are [66],

- impulsive, hot headed personalities;

- lack empathy;

- have difficulty conforming to rules; and

- have positive attitudes towards violence

Victims

A as the second member of the bullying triad, a victim is a child who becomes the target of bullying [2]. The victimisation of one child by another is largely dependent on their relationship. The relationship between the victim and the bully exists prior to bullying [14]. This relationship is characterized by one clear predictor of bullying which is reciprocated dislike or animosity. Potential bullies, actualize angry behavior towards low status peers whom they already dislike and who dislike them [38]. Bullying is not about anger, or even about conflict. It is about contempt – a powerful feeling of dislike towards someone considered to be worthless or inferior, combined with a lack of empathy, compassion or shame [17].

However in some cases bullying occurs when the victim is vulnerable, displaying physical and psychological qualities making him or her prone to victimization [90].The vulnerability of the victims of bullying comes as a result of lack of social support, such as peer relationships at school [66]. They tend to be unpopular among their peers and are often friendless, isolated and sometimes even despised [78]. Victims of bullying also tend to display a response that is perceived by both the bully and the victim as a certain sign of submission. Should an intended target exhibit a defeated attitude in response to chronic bullying, then the bullying is likely to continue [7].

Personality characteristics of victims

While on the surface bullying may appear to be simply the actions of an 'aggressor(s)' perpetuated upon an unwilling 'targeted individual(s)', on a certain deeper level, for it to succeed, the bullying-cycle must also be viewed as necessarily including a certain chronic inadequate response on the part of the target. That is, a response that is seen both by the bully and the target as insufficient to prevent the chronic bullying-cycle from repeating itself between the given individuals. Those individuals or groups who are capable of reacting to initial bullying attempts in ways that sufficiently discourage bullies from repeated attempts, are less likely to be drawn to this destructive cycle, while those who most readily react by perceiving themselves as 'victims' tend to make the most suitable candidates for becoming 'targets' of chronic bullying [12].

Under some circumstances targets may be chosen in what may be a completely random or arbitrary process, especially in groups in which the 'bully mentality' may have already succeeded in achieving domination within the group. In such groups the defence mechanisms of the entire group may have already been 'broken down' and therefore the targeting of individuals no longer requires the seeking out of certain 'personality types' to become the next 'target' [15].

Some of the reasons why children are bullied are these; the child who is new on the block; the child who is the youngest in the school; the individual who has been traumatized; the individual who is submissive; the child who is unwilling to fight; the one who is shy; the individual who is independent and doesn't change to suit the norm; the child who is fat or thin ,short or tall; the one who wears braces or glasses; has acne or a skin condition [17]. Victims of bullying tend to be unpopular among their peers and are often friendless, isolated and sometimes even despised [78].

The following thoughts, feelings and behaviors are cited as characteristic of victims [11, 16, 90] :

-being non-assertive and submissive.

-sensitive in nature.

-a tendency for self-deprecation and approval seeking.

- being indecisive.

-display a need to feel valued.

-have a higher than average level of dependency.

-have low self-regard.

-has few friends and is not socially connected.

-Displays anxious and insecure tendencies.

-lacks humour and social skills

-cautious and quiet behaviour

Notably, children who exhibit these behaviours or personality characteristics tend to be prone to bullying.

Types of victims

The three types of victims are the passive victim; the provocative victim and the bully-victim [66].

- ### *The passive victim*

This type of victim does not directly provoke bullies. They are socially withdrawn, often seen as anxious, depressed and fearful and have a poor self-concept. When compared with their non-victimised peers, passive victims have fewer if any friends, are lonely and sad and are more nervous about new situations. This cluster of symptoms makes them more attractive targets for bullies who are unusually competent in detecting vulnerability. In the early grades, initial responses to bullying among passive victims include crying, withdrawal and futile anger .In later grades, they tend to respond by trying to avoid and escape from bullying situations, these escape tactics may include being absent from school or running away from home [66].

- *The provocative victim*

Provocative victims represent a small group of children who often behave in ways that arouse negative responses around them. Negative responses to these victims may include anger, irritation and exasperation. They possess a cluster of characteristics that are likely to disrupt a classroom and lead to social rejection by peers. Characteristics include irritability, restlessness, off-task behaviour and hostility [66].Their behaviour is annoying, immature and in some cases the victims have not figured out how to behave and in other cases they have deliberately set out to irritate those around them [90]. Often this type of victim is misidentified as a bully because they often fight back with the bully but are ineffective with the bullies because of their poor social skills [11].

- *The bully-victim*

These are victims who also engage in bullying because they themselves have been victim to bullying. Their bullying behavior maybe retaliatory in response to being bullied or they can bully younger and weaker children [84].Due to their own feeling of powerlessness and helplessness, and as a result of being bullied by other children and adults, they will bully others too [66].

Signs displayed by victims

Teens may not always tell parents or other adults that they are being bullied. The signs that a teen is being bullied include;

* ❖ unexplained injuries

* ❖ coming home with clothing or belongings damaged or missing

* ❖ seeming afraid of going to school or taking certain routes to school or other destinations.

* ❖ Unexplained aches or illnesses that keep them from school.

* ❖ Loss of interest in school or other activities

* ❖ Being socially isolated

* ❖ Talking about needed protection, such as a weapon.

* ❖ Becoming moody, depressed or withdrawn or having a low self-esteem [99].

Parents and teachers should be in a position to recognize the signs displayed by victims of bullying as most bullying incidents at school remain unreported.

Bystanders

Bullying in schools typically takes place in the presence of student bystanders. Bystanders thus complete the bullying triad. Bystanders are those children who are neither victims nor perpetrators, but who see bullying happening to their peers [48]. Bystanders are the "supporting cast in a play" whose role is to aid and abet the bully through acts of commission and omission. They can stand idly by or look away, afraid to step in for fear of becoming a target themselves or they can actively encourage or join in the bullying, [18;34; 90].

The behavior of the bystanders can encourage and reinforce the bullies' behaviour. The unresponsive bystanders can be a classmate who finds harassment funny or a peer who sqits on the sidelines afraid to get involved or an educator who sees bullying as just another part of growing up [75]. The encouragement given by bystanders or the indifference exhibited by the bystanders towards bullying reinforces the bullying of victims at school. If the bully faces no obstruction in his/her activities they will gain more confidence and even engage in more ruthless activities.

Reasons for lack of intervention

In most bullying incidents bystanders usually do nothing [58].There are a wide variety of reasons why children choose not to intervene. Typically they worry that they will make the situation worse or risk becoming the next victim, due to the fear that children experience as bystanders, which is a direct cause of the decline of anti-bullying attitudes [45].

Bystanders may not intervene because they may be afraid to be associated with the victim, for fear of lowering their own status, inviting retribution from the bully, or becoming victims themselves. They may also not report bullying incidents as they do not want to be called a 'snitch' ,do not want to make the situation worse or in many cases do not know what to do (44). Bystanders may even experience feelings of guilt or helplessness for not standing up to the bully on behalf of their classmate, have nightmares of being the next victim or fear certain areas in school. Expectations of friends may have a great influence on their behaviors as bystanders. As the number of bystanders increases, the likelihood of any one bystander helping decreases and more time passes before help does occur. Engaging in prosocial behaviour is safe when no one else is present as no judgment takes place [48]. As a result it is more difficult for bystanders to intervene if there are friends or any other people around.

Types of bystanders

Various roles can be played by bystanders in a bullying situation [17];

- *The sidekicks*-are closest to the bully and sometimes also referred to as hench men.

- *Support/passive bullies*-support the bullying but do not take an active part in the bullying.

- *Passive support /possible bullies/bullies*-these children are the ones that observe the bullying and like to watch but do not openly display support; they will not openly approve by cheering or verbally encouraging.

- *Disengaged onlookers*-the children observe the bullying and silently say to themselves, "it is none of my business". They do not take a stand against the bullying.

- *Possible defenders*-these on lookers do not like the bullying and often think that they should say or do something but they don't.

- *Defenders of the target*-these bystanders take a stand; they dislike the bullying and therefore help or try and help the target.

Any one of the roles played by the bystanders in a bullying situation is instrumental in the perpetuation or curbing of bullying.

Normal peer conflict versus bullying

On first thought the words bully and peer hardly belong in the same title, for all intents and purposes the two words are opposites [80]. Normal peer conflict is when two students of the same status get into an argument, but it is more accidental and not serious [44]. A peer is an equal, of the same social standing as oneself and any fight that occurs between them is based on equality and therefore fair [37].

Bullying, however, lacks elements of equality and free choice [100]. These authors further note that what distinguishes bullying from other forms of childhood aggression is this unequal coercive power. Bullying is therefore, aggression by a more powerful person which is not justified. The aggressor experiences a feeling of enjoyment while the victim has a sense of oppression [78].

A clear outline of the differences between normal peer conflict and bullying is presented in the table below [11].

Differences between normal peer conflict and bullying

Normal peer conflict	Bullying
Equal power-friends.	Imbalance of power- not friends.
Happens occasionally.	Repeated negative actions.
Accidental.	Purposeful.
Not serious.	Serious- threat of physical harm or emotional or physical hurt.
Equal emotional reaction.	
Not seeking power or attention.	Strong emotional reaction on the part of the victim.
Not trying to obtain anything.	Seeking power and or control.
	Trying to obtain material objects or control.
Remorse- participants take responsibility.	No remorse- blames victim.
	No effort to solve the problem.
Effort to solve the problem.	

Bullying and normal peer conflicts are thus depicted as direct opposites. It is important that teachers and learners know the difference, so they can be in a position to identify bullying behaviours early.

Traditionally the concept of bullying has been viewed as teasing or fighting; however, bullying differs from isolated, transitory interpersonal conflicts in that it involves systematic, intentional prolonged and repeated negative attacks aimed at a person by one or more people, often resulting in the victim feeling unable to cope [49]. Such negative actions occur when someone intentionally inflicts or attempts to inflict injury upon another [66]. The actions can be carried out by physical contact, by words or in another way, such as making faces or mean gestures and intentional exclusion from a group [22]. Also in normal peer conflict, peers are of the same social standing as one self while on the other hand bullying lacks the elements of equality and free choice [82].

These repeated attacks seem to be fed by the bully, victim and bystander relationships. If bullies and victims had no prior relationship to bullying, curbing bullying would be easy. Bullying however, is not based on random targeting. Bullies and victims often have a previously existing relationship that presages bullying before it happens, which if known would alert teachers and knowledgeable adults about trouble spots [14].

Diagrammatically the difference between bullying and normal peer conflict can be explained as follows

Normal peer conflict

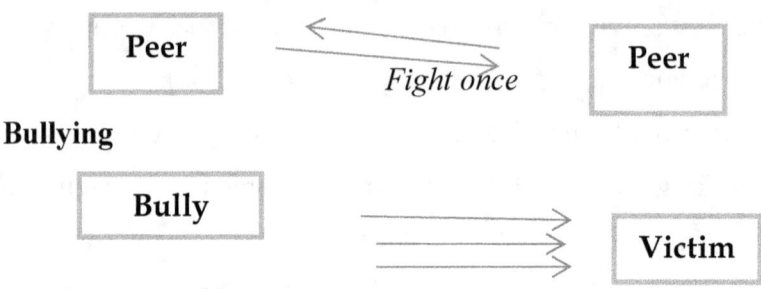

Repeated attacks from the bully and victim cannot fight back.

In normal peer conflict both peers fight because they are of the same social standing and the fight occurs only once. In bullying however one individual (bully) has power over the other (victim). The attacks are continually from the bully and the victim cannot fight back. These attacks do not occur once but they are repeated.

As such bullying presents an unwholesome picture and dire consequences for the peer groups, families, the society at large and especially the victims of bullying [29].Given the extent of reported bullying in schools worldwide and the difficulties associated with its conceptualization, there is a clear need to address school bullying, so that children and the society at large will know when to worry and how to handle bullying situations.

CHAPTER 4

THEORIES ABOUT BULLYING

Several theories have been used to explain how children learn how to bully other children. The theories outlined in this book may not be signature theories to explain the concept of bullying (in fact there are many other theories which can be subscribed to) but they do give an explanation as to how bullying behaviours are acquired

Until recently, most research on bullying focused on individual factors. The last decade however has witnessed an increase in studies examining the social context in which bullying episodes are embedded. For instance the classroom context, both in terms of collective students' attitudes and bullying behaviors, may have strong influences on individual adolescents' bullying propensities [86]. Bullying does not occur in isolation, but rather is the result of interaction between individual factors, peers, family, classroom and community factors [95]. Two theories have been adapted to explain how bullying behaviours are acquired in the school context; the bioecological and social learning theories.

The Bioecological theory

The bioecological systems theory is the view that explains child development in terms of the reciprocal influences between children and the settings that make up their environment [77]. Developed by Urie Bronfenbrenner, the bioecological approach outlines the dynamic relationship between an individual's development (biological development, inter-and intra-psychological development and behaviour) and the integrated, multiple social contexts or systems [13]. The theory emphasizes the importance of many different environments on children's development.

Bronfenbrenner, viewed child development, as a process that unfolds within a complex system of relationships occurring in multiple environments [70]. He states that the environment is conceived as a set of nested structures, each inside the next like a set of Russian dolls [22]. Moreover, in his view, children's environments are not simply diverse; they are also related in specific ways. Thus, children's homes and schools are located within larger cultural groups that prescribe customs and values.

Not only do all these environments have an impact on a child's development, according to Bronfenbrenner, but the interactions among them also exert considerable influence, [70].The ecobiological approach, argues that the developmental process cannot be completely understood unless we focus on the reciprocal interactions between the child and parents, not just maturational forces (nature) or parental child-rearing approaches (nurture), [77].

In his theory the child's development is placed within four interrelated nested systems, namely, microsystem, mesosystem, exosystem and macrosystem, all of which interact within the chronosystem [25]. Children as individuals are part of these interrelated systems that locate the individual at the centre to include all systems that affect the individual [95].

The microsystem consists of a pattern of activities, social roles, and interpersonal relationships experienced by the developing person in a given face-to-face setting with particular physical, social and symbolic features that invite, permit or inhibit engagement in sustained, progressively more complex interactions with, and activity in, the immediate environment (Lerner, 2005). The immediate settings in which children's lives take place are such places as homes, child care or school.

Their daily face to face interactions with parents, siblings, teachers and peers in these settings characterize their experiences and every participant in this systems interaction influences the other participant [70]. This level also identifies the biological and personal factors that influence how individuals behave and thus increase the likelihood of becoming victims or perpetrators of bullying: demographic characteristics, personality disorders, and a history of experiencing, witnessing or engaging in bullying behaviour. It also focuses on the association between family environment and behaviour (e.g. inadequate parental supervision, hostile discipline practices and domestic violence) [44].

Mesosystem- This level refers to the manner in which these (micro) systems relate to each other. The bioecological approach emphasizes that the influence is not one directional. The microsystems are being influenced, but also influence other systems within the bullying cycle [93] for instance there are mesosystem connections between children's lives at home and their lives at school [70]. Hence if a child comes from a family that permits aggressive behavior they may also be prone to bullying behavior of an aggressive nature, at school.

Bullying behaviors have a "ripple effect" [90]. On the Mesosytem level, the bullying act not only affects the victim but all the role players in bullying. It starts at one point and spreads out in waves to all the role players. These role players are the bully, the victim, the parents, others at school and the wider community [93]. What a child learns from others, what they are exposed to during their development, their system of values, and the factors that influence their lives from adult figures to peers and the community at large all have a bearing towards how the child will behave towards others. As a result the child's bullying behavior results from this reciprocal influence between these systems.

Exosystem- This level focuses on the organizational or institutional factors that shape or structure the environment within which the individual exists and in which interpersonal relations occur. These aspects can be rules, policies and acceptable behaviour within more formal organizations [42]. These formal organizations can be schools [24], parents' work place, the media, the school board and the school's bullying policy [93]. The school board is part of the child's exosystem because board members construct curricula for the child's education, determine what books will be in the library, and so forth.

In similar fashion, the parents' workplaces and economic status determine the hours during which they will be available to the child, what mood they will be in when they interact with the child, and so on. For example, poverty and unemployment cause psychological distress in parents, which in turn decreases their capacity for supportive, consistent parenting [77]. As a result children may experience adjustment problems both at home and at school (Evans, 2004), which could explain bullying behaviours. Teachers and other adults who supervise children in school can inadvertently enable bullying when they create pockets of unsupervised times and spaces where bullying can easily occur and by being unresponsive to the reports of victims and onlookers to incidents of bullying [64]. Although the child is not directly involved in the exosystem, changes in this system could affect his or her development [93].

Macrosystem- This system is the overarching system surrounding the other systems. It includes the cultural and ideological values of society, politics and policies [93], for instance the unresponsiveness of the criminal justice system and trade unions, social and cultural norms regarding gender roles, the social acceptability of bullying and violence [42]. These broad societal factors at the community level help to create a climate in which bullying is encouraged or inhibited [24]. The macrosystem also reflects the shared assumptions of how things should be done and how systems should interact on the other levels [93].

Chronosystem- Bronfenbrenner [70] understood that all these aspects of children's environments (i.e. microsystem, mesosystem, exosystem and macrosystem) are undergoing change over time and gave the name chronosystem to this aspect of his model. These changes on the environment have an effect on the child [77]. Bronfenbrenner also recognized that changes might occur in children themselves as they grow older or from historical events such as war or natural disasters, [70]. A change in any of these systems means the status quo has been upset. Children therefore have to adjust to this new state of affairs. How they adjust may also depend on personal development, such that if there is a culture of bullying in their schools or any condition which may permit aggressive behavior, it is inevitable that some children will become either bullies or victims.

Bronfenbrenner's bioecological approach shows how, bullying is encouraged and/or inhibited as a result of the complex relationship between the individual, family, peer group, school, community and culture [95]. When designing prevention and intervention strategies, it should be kept in mind that change in one part of the system affects that system and all the systems as a whole [93].

The social learning theory

Social learning theorists maintain that learning results from observing other people in the social context [52]. In particular Bandura's (1986) model of **reciprocal determinism** holds that cognition, behaviour and environment influence each other. That is interaction between what we do (our behaviour), what we think (our cognition) and what we are exposed to (our environment) [60].If children are exposed to high levels of bullying at school they may begin to think that conflict can be solved through aggression. These thoughts or cognition increase the likelihood of aggressive behaviour. The aggressive behaviour in turn affects the social environment or the school context [60]. This vicious cycle of escalating aggressive behaviour and angering thoughts may result in increased bullying which can have unpleasant consequences.

Observational learning- observational learning is the view that we learn by observing and imitating another person known as a model [52].Bandura emphasises the role of observational learning or imitating the behavior of others in social contexts. He believes that people learn from role models to whom they are exposed in their families and communities [60]. Observational learning, however, can occur without immediate imitation of the model, for instance children often observe the behaviour of adults or peers but do not imitate or behave in that fashion until at a later period when they find themselves in a similar situation or reach a stage when the behaviour is appropriate [52]. Similarly school children tend to engage in bullying activities where there is a permissive atmosphere for such behavior in their classrooms or schools.

Bandura described four main processes that are involved in observational learning: *attention, retention, motor reproduction and reinforcement [6].*

Attention- attention is the first process that must occur for observational learning to take place. In order to reproduce a model's behaviour one must attend to what the model is saying or doing [42]. Two primary factors are involved in securing the attention of the observer; the characteristics of the model and the characteristics of the observer. For example, models who are similar to the observer in terms of sex, age group and ethnicity are likely to be effective compared to models who differ from the observer on these variables. Sometimes, the power and charisma of the model may be more important than similarity per se and competent models are more effective than those who lack expertise [52]. Warm, powerful, atypical people command more attention than do cold, weak, typical people [42].

School children may feel that they should be associated with powerful learners even though they are bullies than with the weak, typical victims or bystanders. With regard to the characteristics of the observer, he or she must be able to attend to the model [52]. The child will only attend to actions that they feel they may be able to perform.

Retention- retention is the second process required for observational learning to occur. The observer must be able to symbolically code and retain the information observed. Symbolic coding refers to procedures employed to organize information so that it can be retained with ease [52]. To reproduce the model's actions, you must code the information and keep it in memory so that you can retrieve it. For instance a simple verbal description, or a vivid image of what the model did, assists retention [42]. Learners who engage in bullying activities could be reproducing behaviour that they have witnessed in their environment, i.e., the school, home, media etc.

Motor reproduction- motor reproduction is the process of imitating the model's actions. People might pay attention to a model and code in memory what they have seen, but limitations in motor development might make it difficult to reproduce the model's action [42]. The observer must have the physical capabilities to repeat the model's actions [52]. Likewise children will only imitate bullying behaviour if they are able to carry it out.

Reinforcement – reinforcement or incentive conditions is the final component of observational learning. Reinforcement refers to the conditions that will motivate the observer to reproduce the acquired behaviour pattern. Studies suggest that people are more likely to imitate a violent model if the actions are perceived as justified or if they are rewarded for their violent acts [52]. On many occasions, people may attend to what the model says, or does, retain the information in memory and possess the motor capabilities to perform the action but might fail to repeat the behaviour because of inadequate reinforcement [52]. Children may need practice to refine their skills, but they can acquire basic know-how through observation. Children can also let these skills lie latent. For example children and adults are not likely to imitate aggressive behaviour unless they are provoked or they believe they are more likely to be rewarded than punished for aggressive behaviour [77].

The importance of reinforcement was demonstrated in one of Bandura's early studies, in which children who had seen a model punished for aggression reproduced the model's aggression only when they were offered an incentive to do so [42]. Learners at school may engage in bullying activities because there is social status/prestige to be gained. Becoming a powerful person or being associated with one at school, may be all the reinforcement one needs to engage in bullying activities. Observation does not occur because of direct reinforcement. Children can learn without engaging in overt responses at all. Learning will occur so long as children pay attention to the behavior of others. Once children are a few years old, observational learning becomes intentional [77].

Children do not merely imitate behaviour passively. Cognition plays a central role in social learning theory. Learning alerts children's mental representation of the environment and influences their belief in their ability to change the environment. Children choose whether or not to show the behaviours learned without necessarily being directly reinforced. Their values and expectations of reinforcement also affect whether they will imitate the behaviour they observe [77]. In line with the social-learning theory, adolescents may observe that classmates, who bully, despite the dominant antibullying attitudes in class, are rewarded for that behavior, such as by an increase in social status or dominance [72]. Observing these rewards may serve as reinforcement for other adolescents to also engage in this behavior. In this respect, the classroom behavior can mediate the link between classroom attitudes and individual bullying [86].

Studies on the broader area of aggression, as well as on bullying, reveal that group norms are related to individuals' intention to aggress or bully [57]. Other studies show that group norms influence the extent to which children or adolescents find bullying or aggression acceptable [61].

There are several mechanisms where by classroom norms could influence an individual's behaviors [86]. Through observation, individuals may learn that aggression or bullying others is rewarding as it may lead to increased social status or dominance within the class [72].Adolescents may desire to befriend a valued peer and could take over beliefs and behaviours of that peer to increase the likelihood of actually becoming friends [53]. Adolescents could also imitate the behavior and beliefs of peers that exemplify the identity they want to hold [26]. The table below summarises Bandura's model of observational learning.

No one theory can explain the concept of bullying. Several authors/ researchers subscribe to different theories. However bullying always has a cause and occurs in context. If one observes carefully they will note that there are situations that allow bullying to take place and some that do not. Similarly there are many causes of bullying as outlined by different researchers, and I have attempted to explain some of them below.

Causes of bullying

There is no one single causal factor for bullying, a number of factors contribute to bullying behaviors.

- ### In-born temperaments

Children differ in temperament soon after birth and these characteristics show some stability throughout one's life [63]. Learners with impulsive temperaments are inclined to develop into a bully because of their behavior [67]. Genetic inborn temperaments are a factor which results in certain children becoming bullies [17]. With regard to inborn temperaments, some bullies are born with what is commonly called a behavioral control disorder. They are seen as emotional raw nerves that misunderstand interaction with others and justify their behaviors as they react to perceived threats [69].

Once normal interaction is misunderstood it could end-up resulting in bullying. One study [18] confirms that there is an association between conduct problems and bullying, and youth who are bully-victims have the highest levels of conduct –disordered behavior. One of the DSM-IV-TR criteria for conduct disorder is "often bullies, threatens or intimidates others. As an inborn temperament, conduct disorders may predispose these children to have a higher tendency towards bullying others.

- *Family issues*

The environment within the home and the nature of relationships among family members may also be a cause of bullying. Bullies typically come from families with low cohesion, little warmth, absent fathers, high power needs, permit aggressive behavior, physical abuse, poor family functioning and authoritarian parenting [27]. Bully-victims come from families with physical abuse, domestic violence, hostile mothers, powerless mothers, uninvolved parents, neglect, low warmth, inconsistent discipline and negative environment. Youth who bully others consistently report family conflict and poor parental monitoring [18]. Notably, families that are not warm and loving and in which feelings are not shared are more likely to have children who bully either within the family home or in other locations in which the children meet others [107].

- *The school context*

The school provides the first location of socialization away from the family unit, where a child can be exposed to ideas of variance with those learned at home and where choices of behavior and companions must be made without dependence on parents [94]. At school children also enter a new social environment and have to establish social relationships with classmates [28].The choices learners make and the kind of relationships they establish with others may determine an atmosphere which could be pro or anti-bullying behaviors.

The school climate is substantially related to bullying and victimisation [68] and research suggests that bullying is a group phenomenon, taking place in social groups such as school classes [86]. The authors also note that up to 85% of all class members may in one way or another be involved in bullying. Whereas many of the children and adolescents hold a negative attitude toward bullying, they are nevertheless directly or indirectly involved in bullying. The explanation to this paradox is that children and adolescents' behavior is not only guided by their individual attitude but maybe substantially affected by the social context (i.e., the classroom) in which they are embedded [85]. Attitudes at the classroom level may be important and may partly predict whether individuals are more likely to be involved in bullying. That is, when a class as a whole holds a permissive attitude toward bullying, a student may be more inclined to become involved in bullying compared to a student within a class that is characterized by a non-permissive attitude. Thus the general level of bullying inside a class may influence an individual's behavior [86].

Classroom and school climates are built by the relationships peers have with one another and to their teachers. These interpersonal bonds need to be healthy or bullying and anti-social behavior can overpower the learning environment. If the relationships produce an autocratic atmosphere with a dominant group leader and a strongly hierarchical structure, even children who are not themselves bullies will form pro-bullying attitudes in classrooms where bullies are popular, feeding a vicious cycle of bullying reinforcement and failure to stand up for victims of harassment[1].

Teacher attitudes in the school can also contribute to the high prevalence of bullying in schools. Some authors [39] note that when adults in a school system ignore bullying or feel that bullying is just "kids being kids" then higher levels of bullying will exist. In some cases bullying can be perpetrated by teachers and the school itself, if there is an inherent power differential in the system that can easily predispose to subtle or covert abuse, humiliation or exclusion - even while maintaining overt commitments to anti-bullying policies [103].

Even though schools may preach anti-bullying policies some teachers tease, threaten or intimidate students to maintain control of their classroom, raising the fear and anxiety of the learners [55]. Most schools allow teachers or parents to bully or vice-versa, creating an inappropriate role model for their children). [31]. If teachers ignore bullying it may encourage bullying within the school since learners know that nothing will be done. The perpetration of bullying by teachers is even worse as it may lead to intensified bullying among learners, some of which may accept bullying as the unwritten norm of the school. Schools where high levels of bullying exist are schools that have a negative and punitive school climate. In such cases negative behavior gets the most attention and encourages the formation of cliques and bullying [94].

In a school context many young people view the school as a necessary evil that must be endured but in which they are not bound to take an active interest. Some learners become bullies because of boredom, jealousy and frustration. However, when students are challenged and motivated to do well in school, engagement in bullying and victimization is lower (44). Apparently students involved in bullying and victimization are less academically engaged [54] and the school plays a key role in establishing risk of victimization [51] if the learners' energies are not directed in positive educational activities.

- *Cultural causes*

In a culture that is fascinated with winning power and violence, it is unrealistic to expect that people will not be influenced to seek power through violence in their own lives [105]. The website further stipulates that research points to the World Wrestling Federation (WWF) as glorification of bullies in the name of entertainment and point that the high rate of domestic violence means that many young people grow up expecting that violence is an acceptable way to get what one wants. Decades of research have examined the question of whether or not exposure to violent video games, television and film are associated with greater levels of aggression [29]. A meta-analysis of these studies clearly supports the fact that media violence is correlated with aggressive and anti-social behavior [44].

As children grow up witnessing the culture of violence and bullying, this culture extends to schools. The following as predominantly violent offences in South African schools [88]

- Sexual violence (e.g. rape)

- Drug/alcohol abuse

- Crime (e.g. murder and vandalism)

- Racial/cultural tensions

- Punishment(emotional/physical abuse in the form of threats of violence)

She concludes that many learners become so immune to violent action they see violence as an acceptable form of expression and a way of channeling their emotions. Bullying as a form of violence runs through this hierarchy of predominantly violent deeds like a golden thread [47].The culture of violence is imitated in the community and transferred by learners to school, leading to a high prevalence of bullying.

- *Social issues*

Social recognition for negative than for positive actions can also contribute to reasons why people bully. Situation comedies and reality television, as well as real life situations in schools, for example, show that acting out is more likely to get noticed, than behaving oneself civilly and courteously [108] .Learners may thus engage in bullying activities because they are seeking attention which affords them a high status in the school. Among a subset of bully perpetrators there are students who are perceived as popular and cool. This popularity status affords them high social standing which contributes to their ability to bully and manipulate others [81].

No single cause can be attributed to be the basis of bullying. Bullying is a complex phenomenon and several issues can cause bullying as outlined above. Parents and other concerned adults would do well to consider all the reasons given above as to why learners develop bullying behaviours, especially if they are to come up with feasible intervention and anti-bullying strategies at school or even preventing the occurrence of bullying behaviours in their children.

CHAPTER 5

THE EFFECTS OF BULLYING

Bullying as an unwholesome experience has detrimental effects on the individuals involved. Research suggests adverse short and long term effects that school bullying can have on all the role players [87], and such effects are not only limited to physical harm but also include psychological problems [47]. The victims of bullying, teachers and parents are concerned about the prevalence and nature of bullying and would do well to be knowledgeable about its impact on all the role players.

The bully's future

 Research has found that many bullies embark on a 'downward spiraling course' for the rest of their lives because of their inability to deal with conflict and violence [31].

-their bullying behaviours can interfere with their learning, friendships, work, intimate relationships, income, physical and mental health.

- they are more likely to become antisocial as adults and have difficulty creating close relationships.

-male bullies are more likely to batter and bash their wives, abuse their children, abuse alcohol and drugs.

-female bullies tend to lose their friends

-bully dropouts are more likely to have a criminal record by the time they are 24.

-the bully who is successful in his career can be tripped up later on, when the impact is greater.

-they are more likely to create another generation of bullies.

Children who bully are more likely than their peers to get into frequent fights, be injured in a fight, vandalize property, steal property, drink alcohol, smoke, be truant from school, drop out of school, and carry a weapon to school [54]. Sadly, bullies end up being losers in a big way [31].

Physical effects on the victim

The consequences of bullying on the victims can either be long term or short term and can be very fatal. Victims of bullying may suffer from the following physical effects (44):

- high levels of stress and anxiety;

- frequent illnesses such as viral infections, especially flu and glandular fever, colds, cough or chest infections;

- aches and pains in joints and muscles with no obvious cause. Often these do not go away or respond to treatment;

- Headaches and migraines;

- Tiredness, exhaustion, constant fatigue;

- Sleeplessness, nightmares, waking early, wakes up more tired;

- Flashbacks and replays, obsess about the bullying;

- Irritable bowel syndrome;

- Problems with the skin such as eczema, athlete's foot, ulcers;

- Poor concentration;

- Intermittently functioning memory, forgetfulness with day to day things;

- Swearing, trembling, shaking, palpitations, panic attacks;

- Bursting into tears over trivial things;

- Irritability and angry out bursts, which is uncharacteristic.

- Being constantly on the edge;

- Shattered self-confidence.

Psychological effects on the victim

A considerable number of authors acknowledge that bullying has detrimental psychological effects on the victim, besides the physical and academic effects of bullying, among them, [55,44].

Those who have been the targets of bullying can suffer from long term emotional and behavioral problems [104]. Bullying can cause psychological problems such as loneliness, depression, anxiety and low self-esteem.

- Loneliness –although bullying may seem like a normal part of a child's world and a way to stand up for themselves it may actually make many children feel unhappy, frightened and unsafe [31]. Learners who are bullied tend to have fewer friends, are withdrawn, worried and lonely. They are less happy at school and are more likely to drop out of school. Their loneliness is increased by that they have a difficulty forming relationships and tend to lead less successful lives, [90]. Once scalded by the actions of the bully they may develop trust issues and so fail to form meaningful relationships with other people.

- Depression and low self-esteem –being bullied leads to depression and low self-esteem that can carry into adulthood. Regardless of the type of victimization to which victimized children are exposed, they reported relatively high levels of internalized problems [66]. These internalised problems cause the victims of bullying to often suffer mental health with high levels of depression and suicidal ideation [4]. Victims have been found to be more depressed than students who are not involved in bullying [87]. Depending on the situation, some individuals who are victimized as children report psychological harm into adulthood, including distress, self-blame, fear and internalised problems such as depression and low self-esteem [74]; [89] . Bullying can lead to shyness, social isolation or a social phobia and anxiety disorders, including panic attacks, depression, suicide attempts (some completed) and post traumatic stress disorder [31].

- Suicide –there is a strong link between bullying and suicide [41]. It is estimated that between 15 and 25 children commit suicide every year in the U.K. alone because they are being bullied. Three children at different schools in Norway were reported to have committed suicide as a result of bullying [89]. This is the most severe consequence for the victim as the suicide may be a direct or indirect result of bullying.

- Psychosomatic symptoms and regression – some victims might experience stomach aches, nightmares, [44], unexplained aches, headaches[4], loss of appetite, diseases related to stress and regression to more immature behavior such as enuresis, comfort habits and nail biting [23].

- Long term effects- the victims' choice of partner, career, social life, physical and mental health can be affected over a long period of time. Adults who were severely victimized at school can be less successful in achieving satisfactory intimate relationships. Some victims are also bullied at work [31].

Effects on the bystanders

Bystanders are witnesses of bullying so the effects of bullying are not limited to victims and bullies alone. Bystanders as part of the bullying triad become fearful of the society and believe that everyone needs to look after him or herself [90]. Bystanders may also feel bad and guilty because they do not know what to do; fear that they will become the next target; are torn between their friends; realize that the target may exacerbate the situation but can't tell them or are not heard by the target; can't confront the bullies; don't want to be involved and can become a secondary victim or affected by poor class moral [31].

These psychological complications can be short term or long term. Either way they have profound effects on the victim's psychological wellbeing. Bullying is a detrimental experience that blows a kid's confidence and lowers their self-esteem greatly even their self-efficacy is altered. Victims go through untold suffering and at times it may feel as if they are alone in the world. This loneliness and desperation at times leads to attempted or actual suicide. Young lives come to an end prematurely. Those who survive committing suicide may have permanent emotional scars, unwholesome childhood memories and may never be able to stand up for themselves as some even get bullied in workplaces.

CHAPTER 6

PREVENTION AND ANTI-BULLYING MEASURES

Intervention strategies

The prevalence and magnitude of bullying necessitates intervention and anti-bullying programmes in schools. Numerous prevention and intervention programmes have been developed and implemented in a bid to diminish the prevalence of bullying. It is clear that a comprehensive model of bullying should include the social context in which bullying takes place in addition to individual factors, because bullying takes place in school classes [86]. In trying to curb bullying advocates of the whole school approach, rather than individual – orientated intervention to bullying, presuppose that bullying behavior may be controlled and re-channeled into more socially acceptable behavior by means of a systematic restructuring of the school environment [65].

The whole school approach
a) School wide intervention

School culture is viewed as the central factor when considering interventions. Whole school development is premised on the belief that unless the overall culture of the school is made conscious of bullying and transformed, then the strategies aimed at improvement and change will not be effective [20].

Several anti-bullying programmes are available to make learners and educators conscious of the nature and scope of the bullying problem at their respective schools, as well as to empower them to identify and support victims and prevent bullying.

One of the successfully implemented programmes, based on the school wide intervention, is the "Bully busters - A drama", [8]. The programme was developed after the initial surveys showed that teachers were generally unaware of bullying behaviors, whereas students believed bullying to be a significant concern. The authors believed the psycho – educational drama allowed students to learn vicariously through actors and allowed for modeling positive attitudes and behaviors.

The Bully-busters programme was implemented first to grade six learners and then later in elementary schools. The drama helped clarify the universality of student experiences. The actors (students) performed realistic and common bullying situations with which other students could identify.

Every attempt was made to involve important stakeholders in the Bully-busters programme. The school principal reinforced concepts by speaking to students upon completion of the programme and explained the school's zero tolerance policy. In an effort to secure a long term commitment to bully prevention, supporting materials, (e.g. information on types of bullies, and strategies for dealing with bullies) were provided to teachers so they could reinforce concepts throughout the school year. Class discussions were held by teachers in classrooms with learners about their reactions to the drama. In hope that students would actively participate in the schools' efforts to decrease bullying, teachers involved students in the creation of classroom anti-bullying pledge, where students agreed not to bully, to look out for bullying behavior and to report bullying behavior. Finally, administrators and teachers made efforts to involve parents, providing information through newsletters and outlining steps they could take to help their child deal with bullying. Students also performed the Bully-busters drama at Parent-Teacher Association (PTA) meetings.

Positive results were reported, including 20% reduction in the number of bullying incidents at the middle school level. The Bully-buster's programme was largely successful because it focused on a school wide adoption of consistent policies, increased supervision and the follow-up classroom discussions.

An approach that involves the whole school is the most effective way to deal with bullying. It sets out to create a caring environment in which good behaviour is valued and behavior such as bullying is unacceptable. If the school's atmosphere is changed the incidences of bullying can be reduced. Principals must ensure that corridors, staircases, toilets and playgrounds are monitored effectively; encourage children to play rather than fight; balls, cricket bats, skipping ropes and other equipment should be made available at all break times. Principals should create opportunities to talk about the effects of bullying and how best to tackle it [76].

b) *Classroom level intervention*

Bullying is likely to be influenced by the social and educational climate in the classroom and school [33]. The way in which the teacher reacts and responds to a child sends a message to the child about what the school thinks of him or her . Teachers can help to create a caring atmosphere within the classroom by; promoting good relationships between learners; arriving for lessons on time; receiving the learners in a friendly manner; talking to learners in an informal way before the start of the lesson; addressing learners by their first names and ensuring that learning takes place in a secure, attractive environment [76]. A teacher can implement the following (44):

- Establish rules (involving students) regarding bullying. This establishes responsibility for each student to those rules.

- The teacher should create both negative and positive consequences for behaviour displayed in the classroom setting. The negative consequences should be appropriate and related to the behaviour.

- Holding regular classroom meetings which help develop and clarify rules for anti-bullying.

- Meeting with parents in an effort to inform them of the anti-bullying efforts being made.

c) *Individual level intervention*

Intervention on an individual level includes discussions held with bullies (or small groups of bullies) and victims as well as their parents, to ensure that bullying is ended and that victims receive the necessary support [65].

The victim should understand that it is not his or her fault that he or she is being bullied. Teens who are bullied at school should do the following [98]:

- Tell an adult exactly what is happening and how they feel about it.

- Try to be with a friend or a group of friends when bullies are around; bullies usually leave groups of people alone.

- not let the bully make them angry; bullies often want a reaction. If it feels safe, calmly telling the bully to stop and walking away may discourage some bullies. Never react with violence or by bullying back; this usually makes the problem worse.

- Ignore or block any electronic messages sent by a bully and consider only opening messages from people you know. If you read a bullying message, you may want to keep a copy of it to show an adult so they know what's going on.

- Get involved in school activities or clubs that have a positive environment.

- Remember that it's not your fault you are being bullied and that everyone has the right to feel safe and enjoy school.

- Talk to a counselor or other professional to receive help coping with the effects of bullying.

Bullies should be informed that they need to learn more effective ways of relating and feeling empathy [31].

d) The Role of parents

Preventing or stopping school bullying can be difficult, especially if adults do not take it seriously. Bullying usually requires an adult to intervene [98]. Parents should watch their children and make sure that they are happy at school. They should talk to their children about their experiences at school and contact the school if they are concerned about their child's safety at school [76].

There are many school-based bullying prevention programmes. Although they vary in size and scope the most promising programmes incorporate the following characteristics:

- Focus on a school-wide environment or climate that discourages bullying,

- Survey of students to access the nature and extent of bullying behavior and attitudes toward bullying,

- Training to prepare staff to recognize and respond to bullying,

- Development of consistent rules against bullying behavior,

- Classroom activities to discuss issues related to bullying,

- Integration of bullying prevention themes across the curriculum,

- Individual and group work with children who have been bullied,

- Individual work with children who have bullied their peers,

- Involvement of parents in bullying prevention and intervention activities, and

- Use of teacher and staff groups to increase staff knowledge and motivation related to bullying [98].

Tailor made anti-bullying policies

A year after I had carried out my study about bullying one of the schools which had been involved in the study called me and showed me an anti-bullying policy that they had written as a school. The administration was very worried about the problem of bullying so much that they had begun to formulate a policy. It wasn't a detailed plan but it was enough to keep them going while they waited for the school governing body to endorse it and make additions. This is how their policy was written out;

School A's (private school) anti-bullying policy

In keeping with the school's philosophy, we strive to create a climate in which every learner can develop academically, socially, spiritually and emotionally. In order for this to happen, learners need to feel safe. Each and every learner has rights, namely: to feel safe, to learn and grow, to be respected, to be valued and to be different.

Definitions

Bullying *is the continued dominance of a less powerful person by a more powerful person.*

Physical bullying: *includes hitting, kicking, rude gestures, extortion, pushing, shoving, taking or damaging belongings- i.e. any form of physical abuse which hurts others or their property.*

Verbal bullying: *incudes name-calling, insulting, repeated teasing, discriminatory remarks(about religion, sexuality, appearance and abilities), threatening sexual harassment and any other form of verbal behaviour designed to hurt another person. This includes cyber-bullying.*

Psychological bullying: *Includes nasty rumours, excluding someone from the group, and isolating someone by preventing others from befriending them.*

These unacceptable behaviours include: bullying that takes place one to one, in a group or via the misuse of technology-cellphone, computer, photographs, email, and internet, instant/voice messaging, websites, chat rooms, Mxit, Facebook and all such programmes.

Many of these behaviours occur frequently, and do not always constitute bullying. In order to ascertain the presence of bullying, the following elements MUST be present:

- An initial desire to hurt
- The desire is carried out
- The action is harmful there is an imbalance of power
- There is no justification for the action
- The action is persistent
- The bully derives gratification from hurting the other person

Procedure

If a learner is bullied he or she should:

- Tell the bully to stop(if possible)
- If this is not effective, ask someone he/she trusts for help(friend, teacher, parents, principal)
- Report the incident- verbally or in writing (not anonymously)

If a learner or parent knows someone who is being bullied, he/she should:

- *Speak to the person who is being bullied and offer help/support*
- *Report the incident to someone in authority (teacher/principal) verbally or in writing (but not anonymously).*

Consequences

The school's response should be sensitive, and we need to be aware of not bullying the bully. We need to investigate the situation. In all cases the consequences will be determined by the severity of the bullying, the age of the learner, prior history, etc.

Preventative measures

- *Peer mediation programme*
- *Social and life skills training*
- *Counseling*
- *Buddy system*
- *Assertiveness training*
- *Encourage a 'telling' environment*
- *Adequate supervision by staff, especially during break time.*

I was duly notified that the document was awaiting endorsement by the SGB although it was already in use in the school. The school administration actually had hopes that their anti-bullying policy would be improved and be more detailed. I commended them for making the effort. There is no greater step towards dealing with bullying than developing or adopting an anti-bullying policy. Essentially this means that there is hope at the end of the tunnel for the victims of bullying in that school.

Intervention and anti-bullying programmes should not be imposed on schools but should be developed with the specific context in mind. Some programmes work well in Europe but not as well in the United States [30]. This may also be the case in South Africa. Intervention and anti-bullying programmes should be developed with consideration of the specific context and should take into account the school's culture in order to bring the right transformation.

CHAPTER 7

HINTS ON DEALING WITH BULLYING AT SCHOOL

Solving the problem of bullying in schools is not a once off thing and definitely not a one day project. So many things are involved in bullying. For a start there are the role players in the bullying triad. Each member of the triad should be treated with consideration to their situations so as not to worsen the situation. Naming and shaming the bully, for example could send the wrong message to other learners where they begin to think that bad behaviour is noticed more than good behaviour. In that case it could therefore lead to increased bullying in the school. Bullies should not be pampered and in my opinion victims should get first preference but bullies may also need to be attended to in terms of counseling after getting a strong message about the wrongness of bullying other kids at school.

The recommendations below are not the blue print plan to follow but they could be useful in trying to curb bullying in schools.

The subject of dealing with bullying at school has not been dealt with in depth in this chapter primarily because it is not feasible to provide a universal solution for bullying in schools globally. Therefore a skeletal guideline is given on how school bullying can be dealt with.

Hints for schools

Every school has a governing and an administrative structure which sees to the setting and achievement of the school's aims and objectives. Better still, the day to day running of the school. Bullying is also a day to day problem which should be handled delicately if it is to be resolved successfully. In view of these factors the school governing body, the principal and the teachers should design and implement an anti-bullying policy to be used in the school.

The policy should have clear rules about bullying and how it will be dealt with should it occur. Each learner should be furnished with the schools' anti-bullying policy. This can be done through booklets about bullying, by inserting articles in the school newsletter. The policy can even be attached to the prospectus or acceptance letters.

The policy should then be used to create a zero tolerance culture against bullying in schools. A zero tolerance culture can be created by encouraging learners to intervene in bullying situations, report any bullying incidents to teachers or the principal and even to their parents and guardians.

The anti-bullying policy can also be reinforced when learners are reminded at assembly points in classrooms in the sports field, the school hall, the bus and anywhere else where there are school activities. It should be emphasised that bullying will and cannot be tolerated by the school. With known repercussions for engaging in bullying behaviour, learners could be hopefully deterred from engaging in bullying acts. School rules should be kept to a minimum, so they are easy to remember and each child knows what will happen if they break them [76].

Children learn from their environment and if they feel that bad behaviour gets the limelight they are likely to take up that behavior. Principals and teachers should encourage and reinforce the existence of a bully-free atmosphere in schools by making sure that good behavior is recognized more than bad behavior. One of the ways to do so could be to celebrate achievements at assemblies [76]. These achievements could be academic and any other extra-mural awards like sporting activities, quiz, debate, scouts etc.

Bullying seems to be more prevalent in areas where there is little or no adult supervision. More a game of 'when the cat is away the strongest mouse will reign'. Principals and teachers should also make sure that there is adequate supervision most, if not at all times to minimize bullying incidents. Where teachers cannot be available to monitor learners, prefects and class monitors should be utilized instead. The use of prefects and monitors is controversial, although it does work. Some prefects by virtue of their position in comparison to other learners they are prone to bullying. Growing up I never liked prefects especially at high school. I think some of them did not know the boundary of their powers and they could make one's life hell. I am quite positive some prefects still do that, but if there is a zero-tolerance towards bullying incidents by prefects, it can be greatly minimized because they know that they will be reported if they engage in bullying.

Children should be encouraged to play and solve their disputes amicably rather than fight. Balls, cricket bats, skipping ropes and other equipment should be made available at break time [76]. Sometimes bullying is a way of settling scores (only it doesn't stop), sometimes it's an issue of demonstrating who has more power, and at times it is a result of boredom, having nothing to do. So if learners have sports equipment to occupy them, they will play and not have time to engage in unwholesome activities like bullying.

Hints for the classroom practitioner

Teachers in classrooms act in *loco-parentis*. They take the role of the parents and young children especially at primary school view them as such. They should therefore be able to create a conducive atmosphere in the classroom for learners to report and discuss their problems without fear. In other words they should be approachable and always tell the learners that they can trust them enough to tell them their problems. Creating and maintaining a good rapport with their learners should then encourage learners to report any bullying incidents that occur in and outside the school premises. Generally learners at primary school are afraid of being viewed by the teachers in a negative light. Rather they want to be seen as co-operative and following the rules of the school properly. Thus when a teacher intervenes, learners more often than not listen and stop behaving badly especially if they respect or fear a particular teacher.

Once bullying incidents have been reported, teachers should take any bullying incidents seriously, investigate if necessary and appropriate action should be taken to stop the bullying. One way of dealing with bullying incidents is by taking time to make classroom rules (together with the learners). These rules will govern the learners' conduct and learners should know what will happen if they break the rules.

Tiffs between children are common and they always occur between both sexes in all grades but if one learner has an upper hand in the fight repeatedly then it becomes bullying. When bullying incidents are reported teachers should take them seriously because sometimes all that the victim needs is someone to listen to them. Every teacher should therefore do their utmost to offer a sympathetic ear to the victims' plea and try to find a way of dealing with the bully without aggravating the situation.

Anonymous reports- one school's policy says there should be no anonymous reports of bullying. However I feel that teachers should deal with reports as they come. Let the learners know that bullying will not be tolerated and deal with the bullies accordingly. That is depending on the case. Measures of dealing with bullying could range from denying the bully certain privileges to calling in their parents/guardians, suspension and as a last resort expulsion. Any step taken to deal with the bully should however be in line with the school policy. Teachers should respect the victim's wish to remain anonymous because after all, the victim still has a life to live at school and they should not live with the stigma of having been a victim of bullying. I wouldn't want people whispering stuff behind my back, even though it really happened to me. As a teacher you can expose the bully as deterrence measure but be careful not to make learners think that bad behaviour warrants more recognition in the school.

Hints for parents

Most parents are busy people with jobs to attend and lots of other business to attend to in any given day. By the time they get home they are exhausted and worry about big things like putting food on the table and getting ready for the next day. In their hectic life schedules they have little quality time with their children. Considering the problem of bullying in schools parents/guardians should make an earnest effort to be involved in their children's lives for instance they could ask them "how was your day at school?". Such questions could give them an insight in to the happenings at school. If there are any bullying incidents it will then be easier to notify the school authorities before the bullying gets worse.

Signs that a child is being bullied have already been outlined in chapter 3 above, but it takes the parent to be involved and observant in their children's lives to notice these signs because not all signs are physical. It could be behaviour changes or changes in the way of thinking. Parents/guardians or whoever is responsible for the children must be watchful for any signs of bullying which could be displayed by their children.

Hints for learners

1. *Ignore the bully*. Research has shown that ignoring a bully is actually a very effective strategy. Bullies want attention, be it from the bystanders or victims. So if they do not get attention or a reaction they want. They are very unlikely to continue the bullying.

2. ***Walk away or avoid the bully***. For one to perpetrate bullying behaviour there has to be a 'victim' readily available. If the victim is not there or avoids the bully there is little chance for them to be bullied.

3. ***Don't fight back***. Fighting back can only worsen the situation because then the tension mounts and escalates to epidemic proportions. Rather find a way of making the bully stop (like reporting to the teacher). If you fight back you at higher risk of becoming a bully in the process.

4. ***Be prepared***. Sometimes bullies just need a response that will make them back off. At times victims need to have answers ready especially if they know what the bully will say. If the bully sees that their attacks are always countered, then they will not be happy because they cannot easily get the dominance that they desire.

5. ***Stick to group***- bullies like to attack lonely people. A group of people makes it difficult for the bully to pick on someone because they are not sure how the group members will respond. Bullies also fear that they will be overpowered by the group and being dominated is a feeling they do not like especially because they want to dominate others. So if the victim stays in a group they will shy away.

5. ***Tell an adult***- about any bullying they may be victim of at school, because keeping quiet will certainly not be helpful. Some learners go through painful bullying experiences at school and end up taking drastic actions which may lend them in trouble with authorities or the law. For instance I read in a newspaper that one boy stole his father's fire arm, took it to school and shot and killed the boy who was bullying him. In some cases learners end up committing suicide because they have no one to talk to and the bullying becomes too much for them. So telling an adult they can trust whether at school or outside school is a helpful and important state towards curbing bullying. You can also phone child line.

Brief summary about school bullying

As a phenomenon bullying occurs across ethnic groups. I recently watched a movie called "shattered silence" about a white girl who was bullied at an American school until she committed suicide. In one township in Gauteng, the 'Daily Sun' newspaper published a story about a black boy who shot and killed the bully. The story was even on prime time news. These are just a few examples. Bullying knows no boundaries as far skin color and ethnicity is concerned.

Learners bully each other in any social context although it could be worse if one is different be it of ethnicity, disability sexual orientation etc. In the Gauteng incident, a follow up article in the Drum magazine January issue 2013, fellow learners said the victim finally snapped because he grew tired of being called names such as 'mshangaan',which means foreigner and is always said with a derogatory connotation.

More boys experience physical bullying than girls because power is attached to prestige among boys. To 'shine' more than the other boys, they have to exercise dominance in their groups. It's like the most powerful, the most feared is the 'king'. So they bully all those that they can to make a reputation for themselves. And because they want their power to be seen they tend to engage more in physical bullying carried out by individual bullies, who are concerned about their personal glory. They usually 'deal' with the victim alone. Although boys can also be involved in social/indirect bullying and pack bullying, they indulge more in individual bullying where they can wield their power uncontested. On average there is more bullying among boys, be it physical or social bullying perhaps because of their need to maintain a reputation.

Girls are different, they do not particularly want to be seen as aggressive or behave like boys. Instead they want to maintain their status (once they have attained it).They use social/indirect means to bully their victims. Their aim is to have a large following while the victim is lonely and friendless. The more the bully isolates the victim the more powerful she becomes. Girls can also engage in physical bullying though they prefer social or indirect bullying where the victim finds themselves subject to pack/group bullying. The victim suffers at the hands of this mean group of kids with one leader who masterminds their bullying activities. The bully in this context behaves like a 'general' giving orders to his 'lieutenants'.

These lieutenants follow the rules to the dot. For example they will laugh when the principal bully tells them to. They will not play with the victim unless told to do so. For the followers, it is sad that even though bullying could be against their will, the fear of offending the principal bully and becoming the next victim makes them stay in the group.

In the case of direct/physical bullying, the more physically advantaged the bully the meaner he becomes and the more likely they are to cause terror among other kids. They use their attributes or stature to intimidate and subdue other learners, which is why perhaps some victims (especially the tiny ones) fail to give adequate response to make the bully back off. If you are honestly being harassed by this big and very strong kid, you will be intimidated first by their stature before you consider their actions. In the study I carried out learners stated that quite a large number of bullies were physically advantaged than their victims; they had bigger bodies and were taller than their victims.

Lack of respect for other learners is the most common cause of bullying. Respect for other people is a very important ingredient of healthy social relationships. Once there is no respect then one begins to overstep their boundaries and does not care about whether their actions are hurtful to other people or not. Sometimes actions are committed with the sole intention of hurting those they have no respect for. Bullying is also intentional and behavior certainly caused by lack of respect for the victim. Bullies target kids they have no respect for and they will repeatedly hurt them so that they are subdued. The bully in turn thinks they are getting 'respect' though in some sick twisted way. The kind of 'respect' the bully gets doesn't even constitute respect because they become feared instead. Bullies force other kids especially victims to fear them because of their mean behaviour.

Several studies indicate that bullying has adverse psychological effects which include having a low self-esteem, becoming a bully-victim, suicidal thoughts and becoming self-conscious. Bullying is infact a scourge to the entire learners' population at school and the school staff, but it does not stop there it extends beyond the walls and the grounds of the school to the community at large. Clearly it is not the learners only who are affected by bullying. The parents, guardians and the whole community where the school exists is affected.

Imagine how you will feel as a parent\ guardian if you hear that your child or some children are bullying others at school. Such news has a negative impact on parents, worse if their child is a victim of bullying. In the school premises everyone suffers starting from the bully who has to deal with the long term consequences of their behaviour. Their bullying behaviour which they could be enjoying becomes detrimental in their social existence with other people. For victims the bullying may never be erased from their minds leaving deep emotional scars that may never heal. The bystanders on the other hand live in perpetual fear that they will be next. The intensity of the effects of bullying on the role players and the community at large warrants stern intervention measures to curb it, if not stop it altogether.

Some victims feel that bullying will never stop. If a child wakes up to go to school daily to meet this one kid who knows how to make their life miserable and adults in the school and the community do not intervene to stop the bully, they may begin to feel that bullying will never stop. In fact the pain that victims go through makes them believe that there is no feasible solution to their problem. Their lives become miserable in the hands of the bullies, so much that some contemplate committing suicide or commit it for real, because the community around them and the learners do not seem to be able to help them. As such the victims' social relationships are negatively affected. They develop trust issues. They don't know who is in their camp and who is not because even though there might be sympathetic bystanders they are afraid to publicly challenge the bully and intervene for fear of being the next victim. They resultedly have fewer friends if any.

Spending time without the company of friends even makes them more vulnerable to the bully because the bully prefers to attack the victims when they are alone without a chance of intervention. When victims lose all the social support they could possible need to fight off or escape the bully they become very unhappy at school and also become afraid of going to school.

Sometime back I read an article about avoiding conflict and one of the ways caught my eye. The writer said that people should not fight back or ignore people who are trying to cause conflict. True enough some learners avoid being bullied by adopting this strategy. In several studies, victims have reported that they stay away from bullies to avoid being bullied.

Learners recognize that bullying can be stopped if bullies are exposed. Some bystanders and even victims muster up the courage to go and report the bully to teachers, parents or any other adult that they trust. Sometimes learners confide in their friends or siblings especially at a younger age, because they need help they don't feel that embarrassed by telling an adult. However as children grow older they begin to feel embarrassed about reporting their bullying experiences so they clam up and some end up committing suicide because the whole experience is overwhelming for them. Taking into consideration that learners do not always report bullies, it is worrisome to note that some bullies are never reported at all. These bullies' behaviour goes on unchecked and they never take responsibility for their actions while victims are continually hurt and bear deep emotional scares.

REFERENCES

1. Ahn, H.J., Garandeau, C.F. and Rodkin, P.C. (2010). Effects of classroom embeddedness and density on the social status of aggressive and victimized children. *Journal of Early Adolescence 30, 76-101.*

2. Anderson, G. (2007).*The impact of bullying on the Adolescent's sense of self.* Unpublished Master's Thesis, University of Pretoria. South Africa.

3. Ayenibiowo, K. O. and Akinbode, G. A. (2011). Psychopathology of Bullying and emotional abuse among school children. *Ife Psychologia,* 19 (2), 127-141.

4. Baldry, A.(2004).The impact of direct and indirect bullying on the mental and Physical health of Italian youngsters. *Aggressive behavior*, 30, 343-355.

5. Baldry, A.C., & Farrington, D.P. (2000). Bullies and delinquents: Personal Characteristics and parenting styles. *Journal of Community & Applied Social Psychology,* 10,17-31.

6. Bandura, A. (1986). *Social Foundations of Thought and Action: A Social Cognitive Theory.* Englewood Cliffs, NJ. Prentice-Hall.

7. Banks, J. (2010). *Stamp out bullying.* Available on **www.youtube.com/watch?v=wzlukEtsgCA** Accessed on 18/12/11

8. Belle, A.V. and Scott, P.C. (2001). Bully busters: Using a drama to empower students to take a Stand against bullying behavior. *Professional School Counseling.* 4, 300-306.

9. Bennet, E. (2006). *Peer abuse know more: Bullying from a psychological perspective.* Google Search.

10. Britske` Listy (2000), June 12. *The school sadists. The horror of bullying in Czech Schools.* Available on **www.ce_review.org/00/23/culik.html** Accessed on 26.03.12.

11. Bonds, M. and Stoker, S. (2000). *Bully Proofing your School: A Comprehensive Approach for Middle Schools.* Colorado: Sopris West.

12. Borba, M.(2010). *Problem solving to prevent bullying.* Available on **www.micheleboerba/blog2010/09/22/problem-solving-to-prevent-bullying** Accessed on 18.12.11.

13. Bronfenbrenner, U.(2005*). Making human beings human. Bioecological perspectives on human development.* London. SAGE.

14. Card, N.A. and Hodges, E.V.E. (2008). Peer victimization among school children: Correlations, causes, consequences and considerations in assessment and intervention school. *Psychology Quarterly,* 25, 63-83.

15. Clark, M. (2010). *Safe schools: Breaking the cycle of violence.* Available at **www.conflictmediation.net/bullies.html** Accessed 18.12.11.

16. Coloroso, B. (2002). *The bully, the bullied and the bystander*: Wrecking the cycle of Violence. New York: Harper Collins   Publishers.

17. Coloroso, B. (2003). *The bully, the bullied and the bystander.* New York: Harper Collins   Publishers.

18. Cook, C. R., Williams, K. R., Guerra, N. G., Kim, T. E. and Sadek, S. (2010). Predictors of bullying and victimization in childhood and adolescence. A meta-analytic investigation. *School Psychology Quarterly*, 25, 65-83.

19. Dake, J. A., Price, J. H. and Telljohann, S. K.(2003).The nature and extent of bullying in schools. *Journal of School Health, 73(5).170-180.*

20. Davidshoff, S. and Lazarus, S. (1997). *The learning school: an organization development approach.* Kenwyn. Juta and Co. Ltd.

21. Delara, E. and Garbarino, J. (2003).*And words can hurt forever: How to* York. *protect adolescents from bullying, Harassment and Emotional violence.* New Free Press.

22. De Wet, C. (2005).The voices of victims and witnesses of school bullying. *Koers,* 70 (4)705-725.

23. De Wet, C.(2007). Educators' perceptions on bullying prevention strategies. *South African Journal of Psychology,* 27(2), 191-208.

24. De Wet, C. (2011).The Prevention of Educator targeted bullying :the perspectives of school principals. *Tydiskrif vir Christelike Wetenskap* (1ste Kwartaal), 1- 21.

25. Donald, D., Lazarus, S. and Lolwana, P.(2001).*Educational psychology in social context: Challenges of development, social issues and special needs in Southern Africa.* (2nd Edition). Cape Town. Oxford University Press.

26. Duffy, A. L. and Nesdale, D. (2009). Peer groups, social identity and children's bullying behaviour. *Social development, 18, 121-139.*

27. Duncan, R. (2011).Family relationship of bullies and victims.In D.L. Espelage and S.M. Swearer. (Eds). *Bullying in North American schools* (2nd Edition). 191-204. New York. Routledge.

28. Eslea,M., Menesini, E., Mortia, Y, O'Moore, M. Mora-Merchan, J.A. and Pereira, B. (2003).Friendship and loneliness among bullies and victims: Data from seven countries. *Aggressive Behaviour, 30, 71-83.*

29. Espelage, D. L. and Swearer, S.M. (2011). *Bullying in North American schools* (2nd Ed). New York: Routledge.

30. Farrington, P. P. and Ttofi, M. M. (2009). Bullying short term and long term effects and the importance of Defiance Theory in explanation and prevalence. *Victims and Offenders*, 3, 289 – 312.

31. Field, E.M. (2011) *Bully Blocking. Six secrets to help children deal with teasing and bullying.* Available at www.bullying.com.au/schoolbullying 06.10.11.

32. Fouche`,C. B. and De Vos, A. S. (2005). Problem Formulation in De Vos, A.S.(Ed), Strydom, H., Fouche`, C. B. and Delport, C.S. L. (2005). *Research at Grass Roots for the social sciences and sciences professions.* (3rd ed). Pretoria . Van Schaik publishers.

33. Galloway, D. and Roland, E. (2004).Is the direct approach to reducing bullying always the best? In Rigby, K., Smith, P. K. and Pepler, D(Eds). *Bullying in schools. How to successful can intervention be?* Cambridge. University Press.

34. Garret A.G. (2003). *Bullying in American schools. United States of America.* Mcfarland and Company Inc.

35. Greef, P. (2004). *The nature and prevalence of bullying the intermediate phase.* Unpublished Masters'. Thesis. University of Fee state.

36. Hammond, P. (2006) *Bullying. A Biblical perspective Joy: Magazine.* 15, (4), 14-16.

37. Hartup,W.W. (1993).Peer relations in P.H. Mussen (Series Ed).E. M. Hetherington (Vol Ed*), Handbook of Child Psychology: Socialisation, personality, and social development* (4th ed), vol 4, 103-196. New York. Wiley.

38. Hodges, E.V.E., Peets, K. and Salmivalli, C. (2009). A Person situation approach to Understanding aggressive behavior and underlying aggressogenic thought In Harris, M. J. (Ed). *Bullying, rejection and peer victimization. A social cognitive neuroscience perspective* (125-150) NewYork: Springer.

39. Holt, M., Keyes, M. and Koenig, B. (2011). Teachers' attitudes toward bullying in D.L. Espelage & S. M. Swearer (Eds.). *Bullying in North American Schools.* (2nd Edition). (119-131). New York: Routledge.

40. Keith, S. and Martin, M.E. (2005) Cyber-bullying: Creating a culture of respect in a cyber world. *Reclaiming children and youth,* 13(4), 224-228.

41. Kim, Y. S. and Leventhal, B. (2008). *Bullying and Suicide. A Journal of Adolescent Medicine and Health,* 20(2), 133-154.

42. King, L. A.,(2009). *The Science of Psychology. An appreciative view.* McGraw-hill. New York.

43. Kristensen, S.M. and Smith, P.K. (2003). The use of coping strategies by Danish children classed as bullies, victims, bully-victims and uninvolved in response to different (hypothetical)types of bullying. *Scandinavia Journal of Psychology, 44, 479-488.*

44. Krug, E.G., Mercy, J.M., Dahlberg, L.L. and Zwi, A.B. (2002). The World report on Violence and Health. *The Lancet.* 360, October, 1083-1088.

45. Liepe-Levinson, K. and Levison M. H.(2005). A general approach to semantics. *Institute General,* 4-16.

46. Lyzickni, J.M. McCafffree, M.A. and Robinowitz, C.B. (2004). Childhood bullying: Implications for physicians. *American Family Physician, 70, 1723-1736.*

47. Maree, K. (2005). Bending the neck to the Yoke or getting up on one's hind legs? Getting to grips with bullying. *Acta criminologica,* 18(2).15-33.

48. Mestry, R., Van de Merwe, M. and Squelch. J. S., (2006). Bystander Behavior of school children observing bullying. *South African Educational Journal,* 3 (2), 46-59.

49. MacDonald, H., and Swart ,E.(2004). *The culture of bullying at a primary school.* Education as Change, 8, 33-55.

50. Mikkelson, S.B. and Einarsen, S.(2004). Psychiatric distress and symptoms of PTSD among victims of bullying at work. *British Journal of Guidance and Counseling, 32, 335- 356.*

51. Milson, A. and Gallo, L. L. (2006). Bullying in Middle schools: Prevention and intervention. *Middle School Journal, 37, 3, 12-19.*

52. Mkize, N.(2003).Learning, in Nicholas, L.(ed) (2003).*Introduction to Psychology.* (2nd ed). UCT Press. Cape Town.

53. Mrug, S., Hoza, B. and Bukowksi, W. M. (2004). Choosing or being chosen by aggressive-disruptive peers. Do they contribute to childrens' externalizing and internalizing problems? *Journal of Abnormal Child Psychology,32,53-65.*

54. Nansel, T. R., Haynie, D. L., and Simons –Morton, B. G. (2003). The Association of bullying and victimisation with Middle school adjustment. *Journal of Applied School Psychology*, 19, 45-61.

55. Nansel, T. R., Over peck, M., Pilla, R. S., Ruan. W. J., Simmons – Morton, B. and Scheidt, P. (2001). Bullying behavior among U. S. Youth: Prevalence and association with psychological adjustment. *Journal of the American Medical Association,* 285, 2094-2100.

56. National Centre for Education statistics (2011) Available at www.nces.ed.gov/cyberbullying 20.08.11

57. Nesdale, D., Durkirn, K., Maass, A., Kiesner, J., and Griffiths, J.A. (2008). *Effects of group norms on childrens' intention to bully. Social Development, 17,889-907.*

58. Nelson, E. D. and Lambert, R.D. (2001). Sticks, stones and semantics: The Ivory Tower. *Qualitative Sociology,* 83-106.

59. Neser, J., Ovens, M., Van der Merwe, E., Morodi, R. & Ladikos, A. 2003. Bullying in schools: A general overview. *Acta Criminologica,* 16(1):127-157.

60. Nevid, J.S. (2007).*Psychology Concepts and Applications*. Boston. Houghton Mifflin Company .

61. Olaja, K and Nesdale, D. (2004). Bullying and social identity: The effects of group norms and distinctiveness threat on attitudes towards bullying. *British Journal of developmental psychology, 22,19-35.*

62. Olfasen, N. and Viemero, V. (2000). Bully/victim problems and coping with stress among 10-12-year-old pupils in Aland, Finland. *Aggressive Behavior, 26,57-65.*

63. Oliver,R., Hoover, H. J. and Hazler, R.(1994). The perceived roles of bullying *in* small-town Midwestern schools. *Journal of Counseling and Development, 72(4), 416-419.*

64. Olweus, D. (1997). Annotation: Bullying at school. Basic facts of a school based intervention programme. *Irish Journal of Psychology. 18,170-190.*

65.Olweus, D., Limber, S. and Mihalic, S.F.(1999).*Blue prints for violence prevention.* Book nine: Bullying prevention program. Boulder. Centre for the study and prevention of violence.

66. Olweus, D. (2000).*The nature of school bullying.* London. Routledge.

67. Olweus, D. (2011). Avail at www.Olweus.org/public/bullying/page. 28.07.12

68. Orpinas, P. and Horne, A. M. (2006). *Bullying prevention. Creating a positive school climate and developing social competence.* Washington ,DC. American Psychological Association.

69. Parsons, L. (2005).*Bullied teacher, bullied student. How to recognize the bullying Culture in your school and what to do about it.* Canada. Pembroke Publishers.

70. Patterson, J. C. (2008). *Child development.* New York. McGraw-hill.

71. Pearce, J. (1991). *What can be done about bullying?* London. Longman.

72. Pellegrini, A. D. and Long, J. D., (2002). A longitudinal study of bullying, dominance and victimisation during transition from primary school through secondary School. *British Journal of Developmental Psychology, 20,259-280.*

73. Pellegrini, A. D., Long, J. D., Solberg, D., Roseth. C., DuPuis, D., Bohn, C. and Hickey, M. (2010). Bullying and Social status during school transitions. In Jimerson, S. J., Swearer, S. M. and Espelage, D.L. (2010).*Handbook of bullying in schools: An international perspective.* (199-210). New York. Routledge.

74. Pepler D. J. and Craig W. (2000). *Interventions.* Youth Update. Publication of the Institute for the Study of Anti-social Youth.

75. Pepler, D., Craig, W., O'Connell, P., Atlas, R. and Church, A. (2004). Making A difference in bullying evaluation of a systematic school – based programme in Canada. In Smith, P. K., Pepler, D. and Rigby, K. (Eds). *Bullying in schools. How successful can interventions be?* (pp. 125-140) Cambridge: Cambridge University press.

76. Potterton, M. (2004). *Beat Bullying. A Practical Guide for Schools.* Catholic Institute of Education. London.

77. Rathus, A. (2006). *Childhood voyages in development.* (2nd edition). California. Thomas Wadsworth.

78. Rigby, K. (2002). *New perspectives on bullying.* London. Jessica Kingsley Publishers.

79. Ritcher, L., Palmary, I., De Wet, T. (2000). The transition of violence in *schools: Birth to Ten, children's experiences of bullying. Urban Health and Development Bulletin,* 3, 19-22.

80. Rodkin, P. C., and Berger, C. (2008). Who bullies whom? Social status asymmetries by victim gender. *International Journal of Behavioral Development,* 32, 473-485.

81. Rodkin, P.C., Farmer, T.W., Pearl, R. and Van Acker, R. (2006). They're cool: social status and peer group supports for aggressive boys and girls. *Social Development,* 15,175-204.

82. Rodkin, P. C. and Karimpour, R. (2008). What's a hidden bully? In S. Hymel, S, Swearer, & P. Gillette (Eds.). *Bullying at school and online.* Available on **www.education.com/reference/article/RefWhat s Hidden Bully/** 23.09.11.

83. Ross, P.N. (1998). *Arresting violence: A Resource guide for schools and their communities.* Toronto: Ontario Public schools teachers Federation. Avail on www.wikipedia.org/wiki/schoolbullying/schoolbullyingstatistics 06.10.11

84. Ross, C. (2011). Bullying among students with disabilities in D.L. Espelage and S.M. Swearer (Eds). Bullying in North American schools. (2nd Edition) (pp34-44). New York. Routledge.

85. Salmivalli, C. and Voeten, M. (2004). Connections between attitudes, group norms and behaviour in bullying situations. *International Journal of Behavioral Development, 28, 246-258.*

86. Scholte, R., Sentse, M. and Granic, I. (2010). Do actions speak louder than words? Classroom attitudes and behaviour in relation to bullying in early adolescence. *Journal of Clinical, Child and Adolescent Psychology, 39(6), 789-799.*

87. Seals, D. and Young J. (2003). Bullying and victimization: Prevalence and Relationship to Gender, grade level, ethnicity, self-esteem, and depression. *Adolescence*, 38 (152), 735-747.

88. Senosi, N. (2003). Violence in South African schools. *Quarterly Review of Education and Training in South Africa,* 10(4), 40-48.

89. Smith, P. (2000). *Bullying: Don't suffer in silence an anti- bullying pack for schools.* United Kingdom: Department for Education and skills.

90. Sullivan,K.(2000). *The Anti-bullying Handbook.* Greenlane. Oxford University Press.

91. Sullivan, K., Cleary, M. and Sullivan, G. (2004). *Bullying in Secondary Schools. What it looks like and what and how to manage it.* London. Paul Chapman Publishing.

92. Sunday Times (2012), April 22. *Exposing the bullies who make teens' lives hell.*

93. Swart, E and Bredekamp, J. (2009).Non-physical bullying: exploring perspectives of grade 5 girls. *South African Journal of Education, 29, 405-425.*

94. Swearer, S. M. and Cary, P.T. (2003). Perceptions and U. S.attitudes toward the bullying in middle school youth. A developmental examination across bully/victim continuum. *Journal of Applied School Psychology,19, 63-79.*

95. Swearer, S. M. and Espelage, D.L.(2004). Introduction: A social frame workof bullying among youth. In Espelage, D.L. and Swearer, S.M.(Eds). *Bullying in schools: A social intervention.* New Jersey. Lawrence Erlbaum, 1-12.

96. Townsend, L., Flisher, A.J., Chikobvu, P., Lombard, C. and King, G. (2008). The Relationship between bullying behaviours and high school dropout in Cape Town, South Africa. *South African Journal of Psychology, 38(1), 21-32.*

97. U.S Department of Education. (2001). Available at **www.nces.ed.gov/cyberbullying.** 20.08.11

98. U.S. Department of Health and Human Services HRSA (2011). available from **www.stopbullyingnow** 06.10.11.

99. US National Center for Education Statistics (2011) Available at **www.nces.ed.gov/cyberbullying** 20.08.11

100. Vaillancourt, T., McDougall, P., Hymel, S. and Sunderani, S.(2010). Respect or fear? The relationship between power and bullying behavior.In S.R. Jimerson, S.M. Swearer and D.L. Espelage (Eds). *Handbook of bullying in schools: An international perspective.* 211-222. New York. Routledge.

101. Weinhold, B. and Weinhold, J. (2000).*Conflict resolutions. The partnership way.* Denver. Love publishing company.

102. Whitted, K.S. (2005). *Student reports of physical and psychological Maltreatment in Schools: An under-explored aspect of student* victimisation *in schools.* University of Tennessee.

103. Whitted, K.S. & Dupper, D.R. (2005). Best practices for preventing or reducing bullying in schools. *Children & Schools*, 27(3):167-175.

104. Williams, K,D., Forgas, J. P. and Von Hippel, W.(Eds).(2005).*The Social outcast: Ostracism, Social Exclusion, Rejection and Bullying.* New York. Psychology Press.

105. **www.bullying.com.au/school-bullying/index.php** Accessed 19.12.11

106. **www.wesleymission.org.au/bullying**. Accessed 19.12.11

107. **www.wikipedia.org/wiki/school-bullying Accessed 24.09.11**

108. **www.worktrauma.org/bullying** Accessed 19.12.11

www.ingramcontent.com/pod-product-compliance
Lightning Source LLC
Chambersburg PA
CBHW071202280526
45787CB00002B/573